BFI Film Classics

The BFI Film Classics series introduces, interprets and celebrates landmarks of world cinema. Each volume offers an argument for the film's 'classic' status, together with discussion of its production and reception history, its place within a genre or national cinema, an account of its technical and aesthetic importance, and in many cases, the author's personal response to the film.

For a full list of titles in the series, please visit https://www.bloomsbury.com/uk/series/bfi-film-classics/

T0347315

For Lucy and Anna

Lost in Translation

Suzanne Ferriss

THE BRITISH FILM INSTITUTE
Bloomsbury Publishing Plc
50 Bedford Square, London, WC1B 3DP, UK
1385 Broadway, New York, NY 10018, USA
29 Earlsfort Terrace, Dublin 2, Ireland

BLOOMSBURY is a trademark of Bloomsbury Publishing Plc

First published in Great Britain by Bloomsbury 2023
Reprinted 2024, 2025
on behalf of the
British Film Institute
21 Stephen Street, London W1T 1LN
www.bfi.org.uk

The BFI is the lead organisation for film in the UK and the distributor of Lottery funds for film. Our mission is to ensure that film is central to our cultural life, in particular by supporting and nurturing the next generation of filmmakers and audiences. We serve a public role which covers the cultural, creative and economic aspects of film in the UK.

Cover artwork: © YiJie Chen
Series cover design: Louise Dugdale
Series text design: Ketchup/SE14
Images from *Lost in Translation* (Sofia Coppola, 2003), © Lost in Translation Inc.; *Marie Antoinette* (Sofia Coppola, 2006), © I Want Candy LLC; *Somewhere* (Sofia Coppola, 2010), © Somewhere LLC; *A Very Murray Christmas* (Sofia Coppola, 2015), American Zoetrope/South Beach Productions/Departed Productions/Jax Media/Casey Patterson Entertainment; *The Bling Ring* (Sofia Coppola, 2013), American Zoetrope/NALA Films

A catalogue record for this book is available from the British Library.

A catalog record for this book is available from the Library of Congress.

ISBN: PB: 978-1-8390-2491-7
         ePDF: 978-1-8390-2493-1
         ePUB: 978-1-8390-2492-4

Produced for Bloomsbury Publishing Plc by Sophie Contento
Printed and bound in Great Britain

To find out more about our authors and books visit www.bloomsbury.com and sign up for our newsletters.

Contents

Acknowledgments

Thank you to Anna Coatman and Rebecca Barden at Bloomsbury and to the anonymous reviewers of the proposal who offered fine suggestions. I'm grateful to Sophie Contento for her care in producing the book.

As always, I could not have written this without Steven, my companion in travel and life (and who did not say goodbye). For their enormously generous support and encouragement, I dedicate this book to Lucy Bolton and Anna Backman Rogers.

Introduction

Mention Sofia Coppola and most people will say, 'oh, she directed *Lost in Translation*', even though that film was released two decades ago and she has since completed six other full-length films (as well as several shorts, a Christmas special, music videos, commercials and an opera). And, if pressed, they recall two things about the film: the beginning and the ending.

Famously (to some, infamously), the film opens with a thirty-four-second title sequence filmed from a locked-down camera focused on a reclining female form shot from behind. In a wide shot, her torso (absent her head and shoulders) and legs (with no feet) are centred almost vertically in the frame. She wears a grey sweater over a white T-shirt and sheer pastel pink cotton panties. For ten seconds, this appears to be a still image, until the words 'Focus Features presents' materialise above her hip and she shifts her top leg slightly back towards the camera, almost as though she has felt the words' touch, then replaces her leg where it came from as the production credits continue to fade in and out, projected onto the pale curtain visible

above her. After twenty-five seconds, the words of the title fade in one at a time in pale blue script along her form, hovering just above the bed cover: 'Lost' at her waist, 'In' at the top of the lower half of her derrière, 'Translation' from its base and along her leg.

The film closes with Bob Harris (Bill Murray) on his way to the Tokyo airport from the Park Hyatt hotel. Something he sees from the car window makes him ask the driver to stop and he gets out. He walks towards the camera (and us), surrounded by others crowding the pedestrian passageway. A cut reveals his object: Charlotte (Scarlett Johansson), shot from behind (as in the opening), her long honey-blonde hair cascading down the back of her black overcoat. As he closes the gap between them, he calls out, 'Hey, you.' She turns towards him and we see her face: she smiles. Bob takes her by her arms, and we see the two facing each other in profile, intently holding each other's gaze, before he enfolds her in an embrace,

her head against his shoulder nearest the camera. We cut to his face, as he reaches his hand up to stroke her hair, then to her face, only her eyes visible. She is crying. We return to Bob, who is saying something we cannot make out, apart from the final word: 'okay?' Charlotte utters a muffled 'okay'. Finally, they kiss, and he kisses her once again on the cheek before each says 'bye'. As 'Just Like Honey' plays on the soundtrack, Bob walks backwards, smiling at Charlotte, before returning to where he started. Charlotte turns and walks away, glancing once behind her, before a long shot shows her approaching the bottom of the frame, smiling, her head gradually disappearing from view. Bob returns to the taxi, nods 'all right' to the driver, as the limo merges into city traffic.

Remarkably, these scenes are memorable even though, or *because*, they defy our expectations: we arrive at a *moving* picture, only to be confronted by a still (or quasi-still) image. As she is introduced, the film's female lead has her back to us. We see her form but not her face. The scene teases us with a sexual encounter that never materialises. And the ending offers no closure: to our eternal frustration, Bob embraces Charlotte and whispers something into her ear that we cannot hear. What *did* he say?!

Lost in Translation ingeniously and inventively manipulates cinematic conventions. This is the key to Coppola's originality and to the film's designation as a classic. In outline, its plot appears to fit several potential cinematic genres: two Americans have travelled separately to Tokyo, each experiencing a personal crisis. Charlotte, a recent graduate in philosophy, faces an uncertain professional future, while Bob Harris, an established celebrity, questions his choices at midlife. Both are distant – emotionally and spatially – from their spouses. The film represents their unsettled emotional states as geographical and cultural dislocation: they are lost, physically and psychologically. Charlotte and Bob develop an intimate connection during their stay at the Park Hyatt hotel and shared experience of Tokyo nightlife. It could be a travel film, perhaps of the 'brief encounter' variety, or a May–September romance, or a romantic comedy. The film gestures towards but never entirely fulfils the prerequisites of any of these classic genres. Some would even argue that the film has no real plot. Despite valiant attempts by scriptwriting blogs to shoehorn it into conventional Hollywood structure,[1] the script evolves organically, while careful, unobtrusive editing crafts a cinéma-vérité take on a couple's encounter in Tokyo.

The film's guerrilla-style handheld photography underscores the impression of cinéma vérité and stresses movement, yet much of the film employs static images, blurring the boundaries between moving image and still photography. It also mixes tones, alternating between light humour and deep insight into human connection. Broad comedy is balanced by moments of quiet reflection. As the opening and closing scenes show, the film often eschews dialogue in favour of image, performance and music. Yet rarely do popular music lyrics crudely substitute for dialogue. The film's soundtrack consists instead of ambient sounds linked to location or electronic-based instrumentals designed to convey cultural and emotional detachment.

The film is, though, undoubtedly organised around the characters' trips to Tokyo. They are travellers on a journey, a storytelling device as ancient as it is enduring. Odysseus, perhaps the first celebrity on tour, was delayed returning home to his wife and son by soldierly duties and dalliances with beautiful goddesses. Don Quixote, the self-styled star of his own peripatetic adventure, sallied forth on episodic wanderings propelled by an imagined sense of duty inspired by an equally imaginary love interest. Bob and Charlotte take up roles in an urban picaresque. Bob grudgingly agrees to be escorted to scheduled appearances, while Charlotte wanders on her own, seeking something she can't quite find. Their itineraries overlap, their paths collide, and they find a temporary home in each other's company. We carry scenes of their travels, like those of the characters before them, in our memories, alongside actual ones derived from our own travels – whether for business or pleasure.

Since travel is one key to unlocking why *Lost in Translation* is not only classic cinema but classic Coppola, I've structured what follows as a journey through the film. Like any trip, it begins with planning, in this case for making the film on location in Japan. The trip really begins, though, as the characters arrive – in Tokyo and on screen. Like them, we stay for a bit – the audience in the cinema, Bob and Charlotte at the Park Hyatt. As they explore the sights, so do we, until inevitably the film ends and we depart, after the characters leave each other – and us. All trips end – some with finality (a welcome home), some only provisionally, as travel continues to another destination. The same is true of the film: it landed and was received – by audiences and critics – and continues, through new screenings and streaming, to meet new audiences or return visitors. Since ours is, in a sense, a repeat visit to *Lost in Translation*, let's travel back to the moments before take-off.

1 Trip Planning

If *The Virgin Suicides* (1999) was Coppola's first foray as a feature-film director, *Lost in Translation* was her first attempt at an original script – a feat worth mentioning given that it earned her an Academy Award and a Golden Globe for Best Original Screenplay. *The Virgin Suicides*, an adaptation of Jeffrey Eugenides' novel, was praised as an auspicious debut, and its positive reception gave Coppola the confidence to compose an original story.[2]

The idea for the script came from her experiences working as a photographer and fashion designer in Tokyo. With her friend Stephanie Hayman, she launched the clothing line MilkFed in 1994. She had become active in the local fashion scene, drawing on her art-college training to take fashion photographs for *Dune* magazine. The magazine's publisher, Fumihiro 'Charlie Brown' Hayashi, inspired one memorable scene – even the film itself: Coppola saw him sing a karaoke version of 'God Save the Queen', and thought, 'I have to put this in a movie.'[3]

First, though, as she had done with the script for *The Virgin Suicides*, she experimented. A musician friend, Thurston Moore (of Sonic Youth), had given Coppola a copy of Jeffrey Eugenides' book. Taken by its original cover image of long, flowing blonde hair, she began writing an adaptation as an exercise, until she realised that she could, collage-style, piece scenes together to form an entire script.[4] *Lost in Translation* started as a short story that is also more a collage than a conventional, continuous narrative.

The short story consists of twenty sections, some only a few lines long, each headed with a title (e.g. 'Blurry Neon', 'Fire Alarm', 'Room to Room'). They appear as discrete scenes, a sign of Coppola's suitedness for scriptwriting and in keeping with her tendency to 'think in images'.[5] Each part of the short story made its way into the film, in some instances with dialogue intact. Descriptive passages find their analogue in visual detail, including the opening 'Tokyo': 'The driver wears little white cloth gloves. The colors and lights of Tokyo neon at night go by. Bob leans back on a doily covered headrest and stares out of the window.'[6] But the story gives additional insight into the characters' thoughts and motivations: Bob and his wife 'try not to fight' on the phone and Charlotte doesn't want her marriage to be like theirs. 'She thinks she and John won't be like that. She was young to get married, how come no one said anything? She didn't really think about it at the time. It just seemed romantic.'

As Coppola transformed and shaped the story into a cinematic narrative, a process that took six months and required a return trip to Japan for inspiration, she was thinking of other films. She told Anne Thompson that 'she was inspired by the dynamic between Humphrey Bogart and Lauren Bacall in Howard Hawks's classic noir, *The Big Sleep*. "I wanted the movie's structure to have all the different parts of a relationship condensed in a few days," she explains. "They meet, they break up."'[7] David Lean's *Brief Encounter* (1945) was another touchstone, and Coppola's film shares the broad brushstrokes of its narrative about married strangers who encounter each other while travelling and develop an intimate connection before eventually parting.

In comparison to its cinematic precursors and Hollywood convention, the resulting script was still short (only seventy pages), leading some potential investors to question whether it would result in a feature-length film.[8] Producer Ross Katz purportedly assured them by explaining that 'Something that is half a page in the script – Charlotte walks alone in Kyoto – is a four-minute sequence.'[9]

As she was writing the script, Coppola had Bill Murray in mind. 'I always wanted to work with him,' she told journalist Lynn Hirschberg.[10] And the tale of getting the actor to sign on to the project is almost a short story in itself. For five months, contacting Murray was 'like a full-time job', necessitating assistance from her storied network of creatives, art-school friends and extended

cinematic family. She left multiple messages on his 800-number. She enlisted her friend and fellow director Wes Anderson, who had worked with Murray on *Rushmore* (1998). Screenwriter/producer Mitch Glazer, a friend of the actor, shared an early treatment and arranged for Coppola to join him, his wife Kelly Lynch and the actor at Il Cantinori in New York. The next night Murray called and invited Coppola to dinner with friends, including Anderson, and they spent five hours together, barely discussing the project.[11] He verbally agreed to play the male lead – actually, Coppola took 'I might be inclined' as a yes[12] – but he still hadn't signed a contract before filming was set to start in Japan. Anderson assured Coppola, 'If he says he's going to do it, he'll show up.'[13] And show up he did – one week before shooting began.

By that time, the production had spent a quarter of its $4 million budget. Coppola's resolve in securing Murray was an index of her desire for creative control over the project and determined her team's financing plan. Rather than align themselves with a single indiewood studio, they sought out foreign distribution rights, first in Japan, where they secured a deal with theatrical distributor Tohokushinsha and then with Pathé in France and Mikado in Italy. They then convinced Focus International to manage distribution in the remaining global markets, and, after Coppola completed the first cut, Focus Features purchased the US rights.[14]

In addition to writing and directing, Coppola produced the film alongside Katz, with Glazer as associate producer. Her father, Francis, and Fred Roos, both credited as producers for *The Virgin Suicides*, received executive producer credit. The film crew included others from her previous film: costume designer Nancy Steiner and sound designer Richard Beggs, who has worked on all her films to date. Cinematographer Lance Acord had worked previously with Coppola on her short film *Lick the Star* (1998). But Coppola brought on board others who would become core members of her team: she selected Sarah Flack to edit, as she has all Coppola's subsequent films, and, as production designers, K. K. Barrett and Anne Ross.

Barrett later worked on *Marie Antoinette* (2006) and Ross would go on to collaborate with Coppola on all her features, with the exception of that film.

She also drew from her network of family and friends. Her brother Roman served, as he has often done, as second unit director. Her friend Brian Reitzell (who was dating her friend and MilkFed co-founder Stephanie Hayman) composed the soundtrack, as he had for *The Virgin Suicides* and would do again for *Marie Antoinette* and *The Bling Ring* (2013). He had prepared three mix CDs – 'Tokyo Dream Pop 1, 2 and 3' – containing music from his own record collection for Coppola to listen to as she worked on the script.[15] In his turn, Reitzell conscripted Kevin Shields of My Bloody Valentine, who wrote several original songs. Shields' contributions became the 'nucleus', as Reitzell described it, the threads 'weav[ing] together the fabric of the music'.[16] Stephanie Hayman was credited for additional casting and

enlisted their Japanese fashion friends to appear in the film, including Kazuyoshi Minamimagoe, the senior creative director of BEAMS, an American lifestyle shop that carried the MilkFed line, Nobu Kitamura of Hysteric Glamour, a popular line of streetwear, Hiroshi Fujiwara, a streetwear designer who also collaborated with Nike, and Fumihiro Hayashi to perform the song that inspired the film.[17]

The twenty-seven-day film shoot in September 2002 mirrored its fictional narrative: the story, derived from Coppola's personal experiences of dislocation and jet lag, entailed travel to film on location in Japan, and the experiences of her crew became components of the film. Murray recalled, 'The jet lag in Tokyo was so bad that when we had to film the actual jet lag stuff in the movie, I was out for two and a half hours.'[18] Budget and other practical constraints necessitated guerrilla-style film-making. Working without permits, six days a week, they filmed on location in Tokyo and Kyoto,

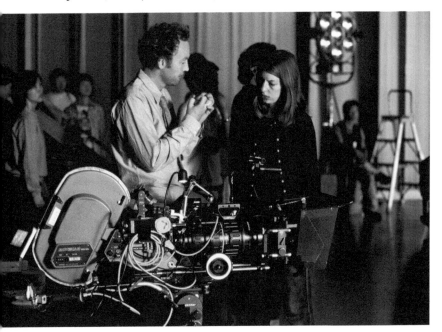

with handheld cameras in actual locations using natural light – in streets, subways, restaurants, a karaoke bar, a hospital, temples – and second unit director Roman captured night-time, neon-lit city scenes. They filmed long shots of streets in Tokyo's entertainment district from the second floor of a Starbucks. With permission, they also shot at night in the Park Hyatt hotel (to avoid disrupting the guests). The experience, parallel to the film's plot, alternated between discomforting cultural distance and the communal camaraderie of expats. Coppola chose the Park Hyatt because she'd stayed there with her family while promoting *The Godfather Part III*, later returning on MilkFed business and to promote *The Virgin Suicides*. 'I always loved the Park Hyatt,' she said. 'I wanted to shoot a movie in that hotel. I like the way you keep running into the same people over and over again, the camaraderie of foreigners.'[19] By contrast, filming in Japan involved linguistic difficulties akin to those represented on screen. Coppola had to convey directions with the help of her Japanese assistant director Takahide Kawakami, as happens in a pivotal scene in the film. As on any trip, the unexpected occurred: a typhoon threatened to disrupt shooting. It didn't, but a restaurant owner did: when filming went overtime, he literally pulled the plug on the lights.[20]

The improvisational nature of the shoot carried over into performances, especially in the case of Murray, who had arrived too late to participate in rehearsals.[21] (He had also developed a reputation for improv after a career on *Saturday Night Live*, of course, and Coppola admired his routines, especially as lounge singer Nick Winters.) But his co-star Scarlett Johansson also attested to the on-the-fly nature of performances. Unlike Murray, she had agreed to join the cast immediately and did participate in rehearsals. (At the time, it was reported that Coppola instantly knew Johansson was right for the part, hiring her without an audition after a single lunch meeting – and was later struck by their physical resemblance. Coppola has since revealed that Rashida Jones originally played the part when Coppola was workshopping the script in an acting class.[22]) The spare script left ample room for spontaneity. As Johansson

describes, 'A lot of dialogue was added at the spur of the moment …
[Coppola] allowed us to improvise, and she'd pull some ideas, lines,
deliveries, movements; silly things like, I'd come in my slippers and
she'd say, "Oh, you should put those on." She was perceptive while
we were rehearsing.'[23] Two of the most memorable scenes – at the
karaoke bar and the ending – were entirely improvised.

The improvisational impression of acting and filming masks
Coppola's firm vision. As with all her films, she had a clear image
in mind, guiding her cinematographer with examples drawn from
photographs – her own snapshots of Tokyo. While their flexible,
mobile style would have suited digital video (and their low budget),
the director insisted on using film, with stock of a higher than usual
speed to accommodate natural light.[24] Together, these choices stress
authenticity – and are key to the film's lasting impression in audiences'
imaginations. The performances appear as the natural, unscripted
encounters of strangers in a foreign locale. The cinematography
retains the realism of lighting and motion – the vibrancy of urban
existence in Tokyo, the serenity of cloistered temples in Kyoto, the
fleeting stasis and spaces of withdrawal provided by the hotel.

The editing process also reflected Coppola's insistence on
authenticity. She watched rushes with Katz and Acord in the lobby
of the Oakwood apartment building that served as their temporary
home in Tokyo and then sent footage to Sarah Flack to begin the
process of assembling the film.[25] After Coppola returned to the US,
she and Flack spent ten weeks in the spring of 2003 in New York's
SoHo district. 'I didn't want to edit this movie in L.A.,' she said. 'I
wanted to see people on the street, to walk to work. That was the feel
of the movie, and I didn't want to lose that mood.'[26] Also sustaining
the mood was Reitzell and Shields' music: Coppola and Flack had a
mix before filming began, as did the rest of the crew, from the actors
to the directors of photography, 'So everybody sort of knew what that
movie was gonna sound like while they were shooting it.' Reitzell
and Shields, stationed stateside like Flack, finalised the soundtrack
working from dailies sent via FedEx from Japan.[27]

Only once Coppola and Flack had completed their edit did they finalise distribution rights for the North American market with Focus Features, who organised preview screenings, media coverage and film festival appearances designed to generate award buzz, as they had for *The Pianist* and *Far From Heaven* the previous year.[28] One poster capitalised on Murray's star status, picturing him perched on the bed in his Park Hyatt suite, in a Japanese-style robe and slippers against a night-time Tokyo skyline. The image, with 'Lost in Translation' traced across it mid-frame, announced the film's focus on travel, while the tagline 'Everyone wants to be found' above Murray and Johansson's names teased us with the prospect of a romantic narrative. An alternative design featured Johansson under a transparent umbrella superimposed against a backdrop of a neon-lit commercial streetscape, with a dinosaur projected on a bank of glass windows above her. The same tagline in this context, with Johansson looking off into the distance, suggested an alternative script: a young

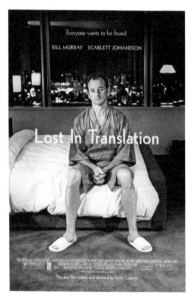

woman's search for meaning, purpose and connection. The trailer for the film fused the two with a micro-short-story version of the plot superimposed over clips, in the same font as the film title:

Bob is an actor
Bob is lost
Bob doesn't speak the language
Fortunately for Bob
Friendship needs no translation
Sometimes you have to go halfway around the world
To come full circle

The trailer efficiently conveyed the dual senses of 'lost' – the psychological sense of being adrift and the literal experience of being out of place in a foreign location – and 'translation' – the need for another to make sense not only of language but life. Through the experience of travelling together, they each find meaning. Or as the tagline implies, they 'are found' by each other. Two musical selections key to pivotal moments – 'Just Like Honey', which is played at the end as the two separate, and Elvis Costello's rendition of '(What's So Funny 'Bout) Peace, Love and Understanding?', one of Bob's karaoke songs – prefigure their connection and, more importantly, the film's inventive uses of music.

The completed film, its director and stars travelled to the Telluride Film Festival for its US premiere on 29 August 2003, and to the Venice Film Festival for its international premiere two days later, followed by a stop at the Toronto Film Festival on 5 September.[29] Back in the US, the film had a limited theatrical release on twenty-three screens in urban centres a few days later, with wide release beginning globally on 3 October. While marketing campaigns and favourable press drummed up attendance, the film attracted audiences largely by word of mouth, succeeding at the box office outside large cities in smaller markets not typically drawn to what *The Hollywood Reporter* described as 'upscale material'.[30]

The early embrace of the film presaged its enduring popularity. Coppola was afraid it would not resonate with viewers. 'Everything about it was very personal to me,' she confided to the *Los Angeles Times*. 'It was a bit scary. I didn't know if anyone would really relate to it at all.'[31]

But relate to it they did – and do. By the end of 2003, *Lost in Translation* had grossed more than $30 million in the US alone. Internationally, it has grossed almost thirty times its original $4 million budget.[32] Released in February 2004, the DVD sold one million copies in its first week and earned nearly $5 million in rental income.[33] Streaming has since extended the film's reach worldwide, over decades. And it has earned critical acclaim. After its initial release, the film was nominated for over 130 awards, winning 97:

- The film won 14 for Best Picture (including the Golden Globe, Independent Spirit Award and AFI Movie of the Year).
- Coppola had 6 wins as director, in addition to 5 nominations from the most respected competitions (the Academy Awards, BAFTA, Golden Globes) and industry groups (the Directors Guilds of America and Great Britain).
- She won 20 awards for Best Screenplay (including the Academy Award, Golden Globe, Independent Spirit Award and one from the Writers Guild of America).
- Bill Murray won 23 Best Actor awards (and earned his only Oscar nomination) and Scarlett Johansson won 6.
- Sarah Flack won the BAFTA for Best Editing and was also nominated for the American Cinema Editors 'Eddie' award.
- Lance Acord received the Best Cinematographer award from the Chicago Film Critics Association.
- Brian Reitzell and Kevin Shields received several nominations for music.
- The production design team (K. K. Barrett, Anne Ross, Mayumi Tomita and Rika Nakanishi) were nominated for the Art Directors Guild's top award.

And more accolades have followed. *The Hollywood Reporter* calculated that it was named best film of 2003 by over 235 critics.[34] On Metacritic, it received a score of 89 from 44 critics – 'universal acclaim', according to the website – earning it a 'must see' designation. The film appeared on several top-ten lists of films of the 2000s. With a 95 per cent rating on Rotten Tomatoes, *Newsweek* ranked it #35 out of 100.[35] *Esquire* magazine named *Lost in Translation* one of fourteen of the 'best indie movies' made in the last four decades.[36] The BBC deemed it one of the twenty-first century's greatest films (#22 of 100) based on responses of 177 international film critics.[37]

Later, we'll examine the film's reception in greater detail – from the time of its original release to now. But first, imaginary ticket in hand, let's fly to Japan to examine the sources of the film's enduring power.

2 Arrivals

While the early short-story version of *Lost in Translation* opens with
Bob's arrival by taxi from the airport, the film opens with the famous
overture sequence focused on Charlotte. As has been often noted and
confirmed by the director, it is a homage to photorealist painter John
Kacere.[38] Intriguingly, Coppola stills the viewer's gaze, prompting
us to look carefully at the image and absorb the surprise that the
form breathes and moves. Denied access to her facial expression, we

John Kacere, *Jutta*,
1973 © John Kacere
(courtesy Louis K.
Meisel Gallery)

John Kacere, *Maude*,
1977 © John Kacere
(courtesy Louis K.
Meisel Gallery)

wonder who she is and where she is. Her clothing provides clues: she is in a state of partial undress, yet not in a sexualised context.[39] No one shares her bed. From the waist up she is dressed as she would be in public – in a sweater over a T-shirt – having removed pants or skirt to recline on the surface of the bedding, as though she is napping owing to jet lag or insomnia or both, the curtains drawn against the light.

As the credits dissolve in over her form, we hear 'Intro/Tokyo', an ambient mix of Japanese music,[40] before the screen fades to black, leaving only the film title. The music is supplanted by faint traffic noises and a plane passing overhead before a disembodied voice announces, 'Welcome to New Tokyo International Airport Narita', in Japanese and English. Auditory clues augment the visuals to confirm our travel-related assumptions. A cut takes us to Bob's arrival by limousine, cinematically linking the characters together visually and aurally before they exchange their first words of dialogue thirty minutes later. The blank, black screen knits them together: the dissolve from Charlotte's reclining form to black implies her descent into sleep. The cut to Bob in the taxi suggests he has been occupying the same dark space, for we initially see him drowsing, his head resting against the window, before blinking awake to focus on the passing cityscape.

Yet the blank title insert also marks the differences in their circumstances and positions. Charlotte is divorced from the viewer and Tokyo, closed off by somnolence and physical separation. Bob's face and expression are visible and we recognise him as an identifiable public figure, the film and television star Bill Murray. Still, he is separated from us by the windows of the taxi which reflect the commercial cityscape of blinking signs and billboards along Yasukuni-dori (Yasukuni Avenue). Overlaid on Bob's face, the riotous blur of images communicates how overwhelmed he feels by Japanese language and culture, and how oversaturated his life has become by the glare of spotlights and commercialism. His gaze is directed sleepily at the ambient shimmer, a waking sensation of dislocation and distance that links him to Charlotte.

It's worth noting that in the shooting script, the scene in Charlotte's hotel room was the second, not the first, scene (third in the shot sequence):

1	EXT. NARITA AIRPORT – NIGHT	1
	We hear the sound of a plane landing over black.	
		CUT TO:
2	INT. CHARLOTTE'S ROOM – NIGHT	2

> The back of a GIRL in pink underwear, she leans at a big window, looking out over Tokyo.
>
> CUT TO:
>
> Melodramatic music swells over the Girl's butt in pink sheer underwear as she lies on the bed.

The change is crucial for the film and reveals much about Coppola's film-making talents. As she said in one interview, she didn't have 'a really good reason' for the shot, that she just 'liked having a hint of the character – a sweet, young girl waiting around in her hotel room – and then go into the story'.[41] Yet this has become one of her signatures, a cinematic choice that carries far greater weight than her comment suggests. Here, it operates on two interrelated levels. First, it links moving and still images, demonstrating an awareness of fine art tradition and a recognition that film is, in fact, a series of still images projected at 24 frames per second. Second, it highlights cinema's unique ability to make meaning through editing, the deliberate collision of shots, which relies on neurological processing to foster the illusion of moving images, as well as the intellectual and emotional engagement to establish meaningful connections, here between Charlotte and Bob. The film's opening is a bold assertion of cinema's status as an art, like the painting it references, or literature, which similarly relies on the audience's imaginative engagement to find meaning – to connect scenes, to make sense of disconnected fragments of information, to link them through memory.

The deliberateness of Coppola's aesthetic choice here may be clearer when considered in relation to the opening of her subsequent film *Marie Antoinette*: the queen (Kirsten Dunst) lounges on a chaise before a towering table of pink and white pastries as a maid slips a silk shoe on her foot. On the soundtrack, Gang of Four sings, 'The problem of the leisure / What to do for pleasure / Ideal love a new purchase'.[42] It's the image of imperial excess conjured in the pamphlets and received history of the queen's reign. Idle, indulged, indifferent, she is the haughty queen who, told of her subjects' hunger,

Marie Antoinette (2006)

supposedly replied, 'Let them eat cake,' an unmistakable reference punctuated by Dunst reaching out a finger to scoop icing from the one in the foreground. She then turns towards the camera, breaking the fourth wall, looking back defiantly at viewers as though aware of their judgment. This rupture reminds the audience that what they see is a construct, a crafted representation, just like the received historical narrative of the queen. The anachronistic music implies, however, that this will not be the traditional narrative, a suggestion conveyed visually as well, though with greater subtlety, requiring knowledge that Coppola's scene is a moving reproduction of a photograph from the same era as the song, a 1977 commercial image by Guy Bourdin for Charles Jourdan shoes. It duplicates the model's entitled slouch as she extends a foot while a maid fastens the clasp of a sandal at her ankle. The 'problems' of leisure called out by the song's lyrics stretch back to the eighteenth century and forwards to our own, via the hypermaterialism of the 1980s, presaging the film's indictment of reckless consumption in the contemporary moment, as well as during the pre-Revolutionary era. As in *Lost in Translation*, a cut to black separates the opening from the remainder of the film, in this case to contrast the artifice of the received narrative of Marie Antoinette's life from the alternative one in the film, which focuses on the young woman's journey from Austria to become queen of France.

Although the focus of *Lost in Translation*'s opening shot, Charlotte is absent as the narrative begins, heightening the mystery of

her presence. When we initially see her, it is at night. Sitting in the dark on the windowsill looking out over Tokyo, she listens to her husband snore. The bed of the opening reappears, as she joins him in it, seeking – unsuccessfully – to rouse him from sleep. But we do not see her clearly until a later scene, where she reclines in the same bed, captured in daylight from a different angle. The scene is doubly inverted: she is roused from sleep by John (Giovanni Ribisi) answering the phone and the camera shows the bed from the opposite side. The shot reverses the opening: the orientation of her body is flipped, with her head on the right, and her face, in close-up, is fully revealed, while the rest of

her body is covered, concealed from view. A cut shows her looking over the same vast, distant Tokyo cityscape, though now under full sun. Her position on the windowsill mirrors the previous scene.

The scenes are tied together artfully by Flack's editing and Acord's cinematography. The twinned shots of Charlotte curled up on the windowsill are static, though of far shorter duration than the opening prelude, and deliberately centre Charlotte between the window frames, as in a photograph. Acord, who had met Coppola on a photoshoot with Bruce Weber, described his work for the film as 'like a stills shoot'.[43] This framing motif does more than merely reference portraiture and photorealism; in sequence and in combination, the three carefully composed shots artfully convey Charlotte's isolation – in the window and film frame, in her hotel room, in the city, in her marriage, and in the film's beginning, which restricts her appearance to two scenes.

By contrast, Bob – in terms of time and action – dominates our attention. The actor, in town to film a Suntory whisky commercial, is greeted by fawning agents who welcome him in the Park Hyatt lobby. Passing along Tokyo's night-time streets, he had spotted himself in a Suntory advertisement, introducing a doubled sense of celebrity: Bob is Bill Murray but also an actor, a film star playing a film star. Cinematography augments his celebrity status: the taxi window

acts as a frame through which we regard Bob/Bill, a doubling of the film frame, a gesture repeated when we see his image framed in the billboard. He assumes an artificial posture holding a glass of whisky staged for the camera. This thematic focus on celebrity and its disorienting effects will become a thread running through all Coppola's films.

He's identified – and as a public person; she's indistinct, undefined, just as her character is in terms of her future. Yet both are alienated – spatially in terms of their dislocation from a foreign culture and psychologically distanced from their spouses and themselves. Coppola envisioned the two as occupying ends of the same continuum: 'She has that early-20s crisis of "What am I gonna do?" And Bill Murray's character is going through a breakdown over almost the same thing but from the opposite end.'[44] He is, in other words, constrained by what he has done, stuck with a calcified image imposed by others, a fact reinforced by his initial appearance at the hotel bar. Two young men engage in a debate with deliberately existential overtones:

[MAN #1] You know who that is?
[MAN #2] It's not him.
[MAN #1] It looks like him, but it's not him.

Acord's cinematography captures the continuum as Coppola describes it. The scene opens with a static shot of Bob, curled in on himself as he holds a cigar and sips from a glass of whisky, an echo of Charlotte's folded-up posture against the hotel windows. But then the camera moves, panning right. What initially appeared to be a bank of lights against a wall is revealed to be a divider along a table with drinkers on both sides. We hear the men's initial exchange as disembodied voices, the shot focused on Bob, who reluctantly lifts his head as they call out, 'Bob? Bob Harris?', and then the camera pans to reveal two Americans with ties flung over their shoulders. Even after they identify him as the star of the action flick *Sunset Odds*, they refer to him in the third person, including while speaking directly to him: 'I heard he did his own driving.' A cut returns us to Bob, emphasising his discomfort, before he stands and exits to the left of the frame. Movement – in the frame and by the camera – reinforces his identity as an 'action' star, only to note how distanced he is from his unfulfilling fame.

Subtly, sound design links Bob to Charlotte as well: the disembodied voices of the fan boys are heard over Bob's image, just as John's telephone conversation occurs off screen over a close-up of Charlotte's face. Both echo the opening with the unseen airport announcer's voice over the blank title card. The disconnect between

sound and image reinforces the two characters' shared sense of dislocation, of being 'lost'.

On his arrival, Bob ascends the hotel elevator from the street entrance to the reception area on the 41st floor. The shot of Bob, visibly exhausted, towering above the Japanese men who surround him, is often reproduced (including in the film's promotional materials), as shorthand for his being out of place. Cinematography telegraphs the message: he is filmed head-on, centred in the frame, and glances up, all choices that accentuate his height and his difference. He is the lone American in a group of men; he looks up

while they look down. The image accrues meaning and complexity when paired with a later scene in the same elevator: a yawning Bob occupies the same space, but Charlotte is also present. Shot at an angle, from the left side, Bob appears in profile in the front left corner of the frame, Charlotte in the back on the right, with a mix of Japanese men, women and children occupying the space between them. Both stand out: Bob for his height, Charlotte for her honey-coloured hair. Unlike the others, who, with the exception of a curious child, all look forward towards the door, they exchange a glance. Charlotte smiles, as though acknowledging their shared definition as foreigners.

Wordlessly, Coppola brings Bob and Charlotte together before they exchange a single line of dialogue.

3 Accommodations

The elevator and other spaces in the Park Hyatt Tokyo shape our understanding of the characters and configure their relationships. As in her later film *Somewhere* (2010), the hotel is crucial to the film's narrative, audiovisual design and meaning. Coppola always shoots on location: the suburban homes and school of *The Virgin Suicides*, the celebrity homes and Calabasas McMansions of *The Bling Ring*, the plantation house of *The Beguiled* (2017), the palace and royal retreat of *Marie Antoinette*, the Manhattan apartments of *On the Rocks* (2020). They establish the films' authenticity and guide actor performances, serving as extensions of their characters, particularly in the privacy of their individual rooms. The Lisbon sisters, grieving and bored, sprawl on their bedroom floor; Marie Antoinette and her friends gossip and shop in her private chamber; the denizens of the Farnsworth school plan secretive visits to the soldier occupying the music room and retreat to the kitchen to plot their revenge; the teen burglars break into celebrity homes but model their stolen goods in their bedrooms.

Somewhere and *Lost in Translation* stand out, for the characters occupy private spaces within a public space – and only temporarily. Their hotel rooms are theirs only fleetingly and their encounters are with others who are also passing through. Even if viewers have not stayed at the Chateau Marmont or Park Hyatt, they have stayed in hotels and recognise the typical components – lobby, bar, pool, rooms – but equally the spaces that effect and facilitate movement (or travel): hallways and elevators. How fitting for Bob and Charlotte, linked by their voyages to Tokyo and their stay at the Park Hyatt, to initially find each other in a space that moves: the elevator. It defines the nature of their relationship from the start: a moment of connection that appears stable, cemented in an intimate, enclosed space, is in fact temporary and ephemeral. Solidity is an illusion, for the elevator moves, ceaselessly transporting an infinite number of strangers from one temporary space to another. The elevator's paradoxical duality of enclosure and movement is key to each moment of intimacy between Bob and Charlotte.

They occupy two separate floors: as a famous Hollywood actor, he occupies a suite; she has a room on a floor above his.[45] They appear to be two generic rooms. In fact, one room was carefully staged by production designer Anne Ross to appear as two, each an exterior manifestation of its resident's interior state. As temporary bedrooms, they immediately convey the precarious state of their lives and marriages.

Bob's suite is so spacious that it appears empty, particularly given that he has travelled alone, without his wife and family. Their absence is ever present. From the moment of his arrival, Bob receives messages from home that convey his distance from them – not physical separation that they seek to remedy through communication, but his remoteness and inaccessibility as a husband and father. He is greeted at the hotel with a faxed letter written on his wife's personal stationery that reads:

TO: Bob Harris
FROM: Lydia Harris
You forgot Adam's birthday.
I'm sure he'll understand.
Have a good trip.
L

Which is more cutting, the formal memo style or the generic sign-off? Wide awake in his bed at 4.20 am, he is surprised by the sound of the fax machine, which spits out another curtly passive-aggressive missive noting that Bob failed to pick out the shelves he wants in his study, accompanied by three pages of shelf diagrams. 'I'm having lots of quality time with the construction crew,' Lydia complains, adding, 'Hope you're having fun there.' He later receives a FedEx package of carpet samples. His disinterest in home renovations is clearly one source of contention. However, his work, and the travel it requires, is paramount in their marital strife. Even more direct communication by phone is punctuated by complaints about their daughter's refusal to eat breakfast, Lydia (voiced by costume designer Nancy Steiner) clearly annoyed that he's 'having fun' while she is embroiled in domestic drama. His claim that 'it's not fun' but work fails to convince her, though we are given behind-the-scenes access that confirms it.

Bob's suite, in fact, stands in for his celebrity persona. It represents his status as a film star and the divide it has introduced between Bob and his family and, more fundamentally, between his actor persona and his true self. He cannot embody the role of suave star, as is made visually – and comedically – evident. As he perches on the side of the bed, his kimono and slippers do not fit. He cannot adjust the shower to his height.

These scenes have been taken as racist slights by some, playing on stereotypes about the smaller stature of Japanese men, especially when paired with another scene unfolding in Bob's suite. Soon after arriving, he receives an unexpected – and unwelcome – visit from a Japanese call girl (Nao Asuka), sent presumably as a gesture of hospitality by his Suntory handlers. The ensuing scene is played with broadly comic brushstrokes of physical comedy and grounded in linguistic misunderstanding, as the escort commands that Bob 'lip her stocking'. Revisiting the scene in a contemporary context, the play on accents may appear offensive. In the context of the film, however, the scene is far more complexly situated, foregrounding multiple levels of miscommunication, stereotyping and, above all, the problematics of celebrity. The audience is well ahead of Bob in 'translating' the call girl's command, which makes him appear as a clueless American tourist. As their celebrity guest, the commercial representatives (who are 'escorts' in another sense) assume Bob would welcome, even expect, sexual favours, and his evident discomfort is directed as much at this stereotypical gesture as at the woman's advances. (The title of the scene as it initially appeared in the short story – 'Room Service' – makes this dimension clear.) Something is 'lost in translation' on both sides.

As a parody of performance, the scene is pointedly at odds with the rest of the film. The escort tries to engage Bob in scripted sexual play, a 'Premium Fantasy' derived from B-movies and Western porn. She acts as a faux sexual aggressor, pushing him onto the bed and demanding he 'take' her stockings. When he moves to do so, she corrects him: 'Lip my stockings,' she implores dramatically. When he tries, she shouts, 'Don't touch me!' and 'Please let me go!', before falling to the floor and flailing her legs in mock struggle. When Bob complies with her calls for help, she grips his legs to draw him towards her. She's like the director of a bad script, and Bob struggles to understand his part.

Bob is, in a sense, never alone in his room. Others intrude, impose on him, insert themselves into his life – a condition of his celebrity existence. He is also never free of his own actor persona, even in the privacy of his own room. Before the escort arrives, he is flipping channels on the television and happens upon his own image as a younger man, footage of Bill Murray spliced together with a reaction shot of a monkey and a car careening through a construction site to create a scene from the fictional *Sunset Odds* movie, in which he purportedly did his own stunt driving. Cuts to Bob's face present him as a distant viewer of his own self and remind us of the difference between actor and individual, between Bob Harris and Bill Murray. A similar scene appears later in the film as Bob watches his taped appearance on a talk show hosted by 'the Japanese Johnny Carson'. The clips from the fictional show similarly present Bob forced to act as a comic in a script he cannot understand.

While Bob has grown wearily accustomed to rounds of stays in generic, interchangeable hotel suites, Charlotte attempts to transform her anonymous, temporary space into something more like home. She is first fully revealed as the form in the opening image when we see

her hanging paper cherry blossoms from the light fixture over their unmade bed. Wide shots of the room reveal the clutter of everyday life: a laptop open on the desk, discarded clothing flung over chairs, bags and shoes scattered on the floor. Whereas Bob is often shot in bed, Charlotte occupies multiple spaces, filmed not only on the bed and windowsill but sitting at the desk, sprawled on the floor, in the bathtub and at the bathroom mirror.

Charlotte, although travelling with her husband, is alone. He's absent even when he's there – asleep when she's awake, hurriedly exiting for his job, or preoccupied with it. John chatters animatedly about his frustrations with the rock band's costume choices while packing his cameras, oblivious to her presence as she steps over them. Even her attempts to draw his attention – asking what he thinks of a scarf she is knitting – fail.

When Charlotte and John are seen together, they are most often in the hotel's public spaces and usually with others. Although not a celebrity, John is celebrity-adjacent, orbiting the musicians and film stars he photographs. This alliance with Bob is subtly and swiftly signalled when Bob passes three Japanese rock stars in the hallway (another public space) as he is being escorted to his room. And, as with Bob, John's celebrity lifestyle is the source of marital tension. He bumps into an actress client (Anna Faris) in the lobby

and Charlotte is sidelined by their conversation, as Kelly flirts openly with John, calling him her 'favourite photographer', adding 'I only want you to shoot me.' Kelly appears shocked to discover that he has a wife, turning towards him to dramatically act out her surprise. However, we don't need the dialogue to see the triangle. *Mise en scène* and costume do it visually: Charlotte's conservative dress, in muted colours of grey and pale blue, contrast with John's bold green stripes and the actress's red top. Charlotte occupies the middle of the frame as they speak but, sonically, their conversation registers as the same sort of garbled babble as John's earlier discussion of the band

(a point underscored visually as Kelly and John are out of focus).[46] Though central to the image, Charlotte is marginalised by their shared concern with Hollywood culture. When she later points out that 'Evelyn Waugh', the fake name Kelly has given the hotel as cover, belonged to a man, John leaps to the actress's defence – 'Not everyone went to Yale' – and chastises Charlotte for pointing out 'how stupid everyone is'.

In the privacy of their room, Charlotte is preoccupied with an internal sense of loss. Close-ups concentrate attention on her emotional reactions. She complains to a friend on the phone that she married someone who uses 'hair products'.[47] 'I don't know who I married,' she confesses before breaking into tears. Her own identity is equally a puzzle. A close-up shows her trying on lipstick and altering her hairstyle, exterior manifestations of the explorations of self she is engaged in intellectually. Not only is she a Yale graduate in philosophy, she is listening to a self-help book, *A Soul's Search: Finding Your True Calling*: 'This book is about finding your soul's purpose or destiny. Every soul has its path, but sometimes that path is not clear.' Though Charlotte looks at the audio book cover with bemusement (as Bob does later when he spots it in her room), the film presents her search for purpose as the inverse of Kelly's vapid musings. A cut takes us to Charlotte strolling the halls of the hotel, where she overhears snippets of the press conference for the starlet's new film:

You know, I guess the reason why I like Japan the best out of all Asian countries is because I really feel close to, um, Buddhism. I really feel – I really believe in reincarnation. That's part of what drew me to *Midnight Velocity* as well, because although Keanu dies, he eventually gets reincarnated.

Her superficial pandering reduces Buddhism to caricature, in a gesture of cultural appropriation akin to the Western embrace of the Eastern disciplinary practices she also namechecks: yoga and karate (which she pronounces artificially with Japanese accentuation: kar-a-TE).

Distanced and isolated, Bob and Charlotte are nonetheless connected visually through the hotel's spaces – before they even exchange a word. The same painstaking, painterly attention to framing carries over from the opening. Matching silent shots couple them. Separately, they both visit the pool – Bob during the day, Charlotte at night – and wide shots link them in the expansive space. He eats breakfast alone at a table before a large window; she soaks in a bathtub before another large window. Each occupies the right edge of the frame. Unable to sleep, Charlotte watches television in bed as John sleeps next to her. A cut takes us to Bob

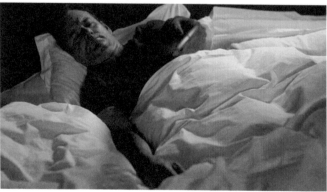

in his room, tuned to the same inane programme. They have been joined – and intimately so – through this matching of their individual hotel beds, prefiguring a pivotal scene of them together on top of one.

But first they each leave their beds and the television behind and meet in the hotel bar. They had been together in the same space before. He sat at the bar sipping whisky at the end of the commercial shoot; she sat across the room with John and his Japanese co-workers. As they had previously in the elevator, they communicated wordlessly by exchanging glances and then through an intermediary: Charlotte asks a waiter to carry a bowl of olives to Bob, who pretends to drink them. Their shared humour is precisely what's missing in Charlotte's relationship with John. When Charlotte mocked Kelly for her Evelyn Waugh cluelessness, she 'thought it was funny'. John didn't get it – and doesn't get her. Bob does, even before she's revealed a single thing about herself. She also supplies what Bob's missing with Lydia. She used to accompany him when he made movies and they 'would laugh about it all'. Now she accuses him of having fun without her.

The words Bob and Charlotte do finally exchange only confirm what we've already seen.[48] They slip easily into the kind of sparky give-and-take familiar from classic romantic comedies, picking up on the silent comedy of the olive scene. Their verbal exchange opens with a wry nod to Bob's celebrity. Charlotte can't decide what to drink, so Bob reads a line from the commercial: 'For relaxing times, make it … Suntory time.' She counters with her own deadpan humour: 'I'll have a vodka tonic.' Then, she sets him up. When she asks, 'What are you doing here?' Bob answers, 'Taking a break from my wife, forgetting my son's birthday and, uh, getting paid two million dollars to endorse a whisky when I could be doing a play somewhere.' She identifies his as a midlife crisis, jokily asking, 'Have you bought a Porsche yet?' He picks up on the car theme during their discussion of marriage. After Charlotte says his twenty-five years is 'impressive', he says,

Well, you figure you sleep one-third of your life. That knocks off eight years
of marriage right there. So you're down to sixteen and change. You're just a
teenager at marriage. You can drive it, but there's still the occasional accident.

She's clearly his match. When she says she studied philosophy, he
gets in a good line: 'Yeah, there's a good buck in that racket.' But she
tops him: 'Well, so far it's pro bono.' She's the Bacall to his Bogie,
Colbert to his Gable, Hepburn to his Grant, Loy to his Powell. Yet,
unlike these classic precursors, Coppola's couple is the inverse of
talky. There is so little dialogue between them – especially up to this
point – that when they do speak, we pay attention. What appears
superficial wordplay is, in fact, the opposite. Their first exchange
configures all the dialogue between them to come – as well as its
pointed absence.

While the sequence contains a few classic shot/reverse shots
to bridge the space separating them, most is filmed from a distance
with the two companionably occupying the edges of the frame as the
lights of Tokyo twinkle between them. 'I wish I could sleep,' she says.
'Me, too,' he says. Ostensibly, the two are connected as travellers
by jet lag. By this moment in the film, however, we understand their
shared insomnia as the manifestation of a more profound bond, their
sleeplessness as a reaction to the dis-ease they feel in their lives and
themselves, and the effortlessness of their joking as a sign of the ease
they find in each other's company.

As they grow closer, they fill the spaces of the hotel together,
rather than separately. John's departure to shoot in Fukuoka
means both spouses are absent, making Charlotte as solitary as
Bob and opening up additional opportunities to connect. Initially,
as in the elevator and at the bar, their encounters are haphazard:
they bump into each other at the pool and Charlotte invites Bob
out for drinks with her friends, initiating a pattern of the two entering
each other's rooms. Bob comes to Charlotte's first, arriving in an
orange camouflage T-shirt that prompts her to say, 'You really are
having a midlife crisis,' picking up on the easy banter they fell into at

the bar. He spies the audio book cover of *A Soul's Search* and jokes that he has a copy, too. 'Did it work out for you, then?' Charlotte teases. 'Obviously,' Bob replies, cementing their union as lost souls.

Naturally, we expect the couple to eventually put their bedrooms to another use. All the elements of a brief encounter plot are in place: they have motive, having found the compatibility missing in their marriages, and opportunity, with both spouses absent. But as thoroughly as the film toys with romcom expectations for extended verbal exchange, it deflects our generic expectations for sexual intimacy by playing with the hotel room spaces.

After their night out with Charlotte's friends, Bob carries her – tipsy and tired – through the darkened hotel hallway towards her room. The conventional associations are far from subtle: Bob supplants the groom to carry the bride over the threshold. The film, though, sidesteps the traditional narrative: he deposits her carefully on her bed and wraps the duvet over her. She does wake briefly to smile at him and, as we would expect, framing conveys an intimacy that transcends the physical. She reclines on her side in a position that reverses the earlier scene with John, when she is awakened by the telephone: she is on the opposite side of the bed, facing in the opposite direction, blinking her eyes open in the darkened room to see Bob's face, rather than the cityscape under broad daylight.

Bob rests his hand on her shoulder – a deliberate invocation of the final parting scene in *Brief Encounter* and a gesture that will reappear again at two key moments. The gesture implies his desire for physical intimacy, as does his obvious hesitancy in leaving her room. He lingers long outside her door, as though unwilling to close it, before reversing his direction down the hallway.

The door – this time Bob's – reappears in a parallel scene that calls up conventions of another sort. Bob awakes in his bed under the same white hotel duvet to signs that he has slept with the red-haired singer (Catherine Lambert) of the resident band Sausalito.[49]

As she sings 'Midnight at the Oasis', a cheesy chestnut about a desert love affair, he tries to hide from view under the duvet, expressing his regret. Though Bob and Charlotte have not been physically intimate (and he is married), this is a betrayal. We do not see their lovemaking, nor do we need to, for it's clear that the singer has supplanted Charlotte (as Bob did John): she had approached Bob in the bar, assuming the seat occupied by Charlotte in their initial meeting. When we see Charlotte in the hallway, knocking on his door, the power of her discovery hits harder, for it takes place in the same space Bob had expressed his longing for her: on the threshold. Cutting between them in close-up, we see Charlotte's initial happiness at seeing him turn to hurt and his remorse. He is framed by the doorway: exposed and caught.

The bed *is* a site of intimacy between Bob and Charlotte, though not in a conventional sense. One sleepless night, Charlotte sees a note slipped under her door:

From: Mr Harris.
Message: Are you awake?

She joins Bob in his room to watch *La dolce vita* (1960) with Japanese subtitles.[50] Initially, he reclines on the bed, on his belly propped up on his elbows. She sits on the floor, leaning against it as they share sake from wooden cups resting on the bench at the foot. Eventually, the film over, they engage in prolonged conversation, fully clothed, while lying on their backs atop the sheets. A fixed overhead shot begins as Charlotte confesses, 'I feel stuck,' and then details her attempts 'to be' something – a writer, a photographer. When Bob reassures her, 'You'll figure it out,' she rolls onto her side to face him. Her declaration, 'But, I'm mean,' makes him, with evident amusement, turn towards her and the subject shifts to marriage. At the mention of kids, a series of intercut close-ups begins, more conventionally registering their growing closeness as each exposes a bit more to the other. They then sleep together – literally, not

euphemistically. An overhead shot pictures Charlotte curled towards Bob, who lies on his back facing away from her. Her toes touch his hip and he reaches down to rest his hand on her foot. Their physical intimacy is so subtle as to be almost imperceptible, while their human connection is palpable. With each other they finally sink into the deep sleep that has eluded them. A fade to black echoes the black of the opening title card that initially joined them: lost in sleep they have found each other. Which is precisely why, we, like Charlotte, are angered by Bob's dalliance with the singer. Not only did she usurp Charlotte's place next to him at the bar, she occupied the bed.

When Bob awakes, an overhead shot shows him under the covers, alone, on Charlotte's side. He has crossed the line. The vacated space next to him conveys that he may have lost her.

Of course, he has not and they do finally embrace before parting at film's end. Before that moment, they do so in the elevator. As we've seen, this public, mobile space is integral to their relationship. They first saw each other there, as Bob reminds Charlotte while they are watching *La dolce vita*. He exits from it with Charlotte in his arms before depositing her in bed and, as we will see, it figures prominently in their goodbyes. Fittingly, it is the site of their reconciliation after Bob's one-night stand. A fire alarm forces them into the crowded street-floor entrance of the Park Hyatt at night. As in their initial meeting, they see each other over the heads of the other guests. Again, their appearances set them apart as foreigners, particularly Bob, who wears his kimono and too-small slippers. They return to the bar, taking up their familiar positions on each side of the film frame, though this time facing each other, a bottle of sake visible between them, a reminder of the sake they shared in Bob's room. The lyrics to 'So into You', sung by the male lead who has replaced the red-haired singer, make the point obvious. They hold hands and try to cover their distress that Bob is leaving the next day. 'Stay here with me,' Charlotte jokes. 'We'll start a jazz band.' A cut shows the pair in the elevator. As it stops on Bob's floor, he leans in to kiss Charlotte awkwardly on the cheek, pausing so long before acting that he misses his floor and the doors close. As they stop on Charlotte's floor, they repeat the goodbye kiss. The doubling neatly conveys their reluctance to part. It also emphasises motion and separation: he tries to exit, but stays. She stays, then exits, leaving him behind. Their connection is tenuous and fleeting. The elevator travels and they are travellers.

The hotel offers transitory moments of stasis, spaces of retreat and refuge to people temporarily staying in a city that they move through – and that moves. The film, like the characters, divides its time between the actual Park Hyatt and real locations in Tokyo and Kyoto. Just as they occupy the hotel's spaces, Bob and Charlotte experience Japan individually and together. When Charlotte asks Bob if he ever switches seats in the bar, she recognises that he's stuck, just as she is. They need to move – and be moved. To do so, they need to leave the static spaces of the hotel.

BOB   Can you keep a secret? I'm trying to organise a prison break. I'm looking for, like, an accomplice. We'd have to, first, get out of this bar. Then the hotel, then the city, and then the country. Are you in, or are you out?

CHARLOTTE   I'm in.

BOB   Good.

CHARLOTTE   I'll go pack my stuff.

4 Sights

The dual promotional posters for the film telegraph its structure: like any trip, the film divides itself between the hotel and its surrounding sights. The static night-time shot of Bob sitting in his kimono on the edge of his bed contrasts with the daytime scene of Charlotte, under her umbrella, beneath a hallucinatory image of a dinosaur projected on a Tokyo skyscraper.

As in the hotel spaces, the couple initially experience Japanese sights and culture separately. Bob's excursions are indoors, a fitting continuation of his time in the hotel, for they merely extend his celebrity existence and confine him to his actor image. On his own, he makes three trips outside the hotel, always escorted by his local handlers and translators: to film the Suntory commercial, to shoot an accompanying print campaign and to appear on a late-night variety show. As in the scene with the escort, they fuse two senses of being lost: Bob's disconnection from his star image and his inability to understand the Japanese script he has been handed.[51] Psychological dissociation is manifested as cultural dislocation. He does not see sights but is seen, manipulated to fit an externally defined image of himself. Problems with translation augment his struggles in transforming himself into the celebrity persona others expect.

The shooting of the Suntory commercial most obviously embodies the film title: Bob literally recognises that something is lost in translation. The energetic director (Yutaka Tadokoro) conveys elaborate instructions to Bob in Japanese, punctuated by a few English words: Suntory whisky, Casablanca, Bogie – and the catchphrase 'Suntory time'. We don't need subtitles to recognise the translator's version – 'he want you to turn, look in camera' – amusingly leaves much out.[52] English-speaking viewers are with Bob, who asks, 'That's all he said?' (Japanese speakers, of course, know it's not and can also share Bob's disbelief.) A simple request for clarification – which direction should he turn? – is translated obsequiously and elaborately, the shot emphasising linguistic distance as spatial distance as the translator walks back and forth between Bob and the director. The time taken to pose the question draws the director's impatient response, another lengthy speech in Japanese punctuated by animated gesturing – at his watch, at Bob – and demands for 'intensity', 'more passion'. Again, Bob asks the translator, 'Is that everything?' This time, the director himself answers with greater animation and impatience that renders the translator's words – 'Like an old friend, and into the camera' – as useless as they appear to be to Bob. As the director speaks, the film cuts between him, shot from a distance and backed by his crew, to a befuddled Bob. With each cut, a dolly focuses in more closely on Bob's face, simultaneously highlighting his star status and its claustrophobic effects. The repetition of the line, 'For relaxing times, make it Suntory time', suggests the deadening routine of performance. The director's repeated shouts to cut each time Bob fails to match his demand for passion (the performance the director himself so clearly models) express their mutual frustration and miscommunication.

Coppola stages the scene self-reflexively, revealing behind-the-scenes activity to stress the artificiality of the enterprise. A rare pan from left to right captures the complexity of film-making, taking in the lights, cameras and crew – whose muffled voices can be heard on the soundtrack – before stopping on Bob, seated on stage. The set is an island of artifice, a manufactured representation of Western, old-world elegance. Bob sits in a tuxedo in a wing-backed chair against a dark wood-panelled backdrop, a bottle of Suntory and a glass on a table to his left. The shot directs attention to the gulf between the American hotel and its Japanese locale: the set is dark, staged and static; the rest of the set is brightly lit, a chaotic jumble of people and tools, constantly in motion. Bob is spatially divorced from them but also viewed at one remove, his actions scrutinised in a monitor. The shot studiedly conveys distance: between the man and his image,

the solo foreigner and the locals. (It also reminds viewers that the film they are watching is equally an elaborate construction, created by Coppola in concert with an army of co-workers.)

The photoshoot does much the same: we first see Bob isolated – this time in the centre of the frame – surrounded by the behind-the-scenes activity of the crew, who busily adjust his costume, make-up and lighting. Again the seams show: we see Bob from behind, his ill-fitting tuxedo clipped unceremoniously at the back to sustain the illusion of suave masculinity. He is on the phone with his agent, voicing the discomfort his clothing suggests with both his work and the place: he wants out of his appearance on the late-night show and out of the country. He does little to disguise his beleaguered state, wearily turning his elaborately shaded and mascaraed eyes towards the film camera (and the photographer's) to pose as expected with a prop glass of 'whisky' (iced tea). This time, the photographer speaks English, not Japanese, and miscommunication centres on the transposition of 'l' and 'r'. As with the escort, the difficulty is less linguistic, or even cultural, than Hollywood. The photographer and Bob communicate by trading in clichéd images of masculine performance. The director asks him to be 'Rat Pack', like Sinatra

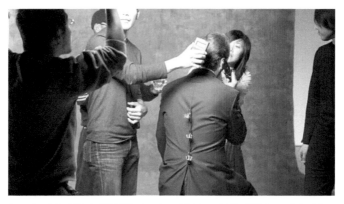

or Dino, or Roger Moore, while Bob prefers Sean Connery. The sequence transcends difficulties with language to skewer the cultural imperialism of American popular culture, as well as its distorting influence on identity and relationships, a theme Coppola would explore with greater depth in *Somewhere*.

Bob's appearance on Mathew's Best Hit TV[53] takes the two previous experiences to new heights of cultural misunderstanding and performative artifice. Another behind-the-scenes sequence represents the taping of the show, opening on Bob standing in the wings on a brightly lit stage, decorated in pop colours, as the host (Mathew Minami) reads from cue cards into the camera. 'Ladies and Gentlemen, Mr Bob Harris,' he announces, before transforming Bob into a prop for his own manic performance, insisting that Bob stand and clap along while he performs a comic 'Japanese' dance, little more than a set of poses that showcase his flashy striped suit and dyed blond hair. Bob is sidelined – literally standing to the host's side in a dark suit with no visible sign of expression. Only later do we see that Bob was reduced to an unwitting sidekick, rather than appearing as the 'American movie star' Bob Harris. He has lost even his celebrity status.

By contrast, Charlotte's experiences of Japan take her out of the hotel and outdoors, a point emphasised by cuts from Bob's appearances. After the Suntory shoot, we cut to Charlotte, studying the map of the subway before visiting Jogan-ji temple. She takes her place alongside the other riders in the crowded car, looking with fascination at the pages of a male passenger's manga[54] and at her surroundings as she ascends the escalator to street level. Close-ups of her face show her wonder as much as confusion. Unlike Bob, hers is not linguistic but spatial dislocation, a temporary loss of direction – in Japan and in life. However, she does not appear as disconnected or isolated as Bob. She is pictured among the crowds, not apart from them. Though she later tells her friend Lauren that 'she didn't feel anything' after seeing the chanting monks, the film suggests otherwise. As she ascends the escalator the sounds of chiming bells overlap with the ambient chatter of subway announcements in Japanese, and are mixed with electronic music, a sonic bridge that sutures Charlotte into her surroundings. She is framed at the door of the temple, as Bob is off stage, but moves inward. Although she is still distant and apart from the monks, she is drawn towards them, rather than stationed, as Bob is, apart from the Japanese film and photography crews. Close-ups capture her actual reactions, rather than artificial performances of emotion (intensity, passion) or masculinity (Bogie, Rat Pack, James Bond).

Movement characterises each of Charlotte's excursions. She wanders and explores, the physical manifestation of her intellectual search for purpose through philosophy (and self-help). In contrast to the stasis associated with the American hotel, Japan is constantly moving: neon lights flash and twirl, pedestrians cross busy streets, and cars stream along them. Subways speed underground, trains above. Spaces are kinetic: monks bow and chant in the temple, gamers play to blaring techno chatter from arcade machines (and they are linked when one player beats a drum to make animated figures dance). As she strolls through an arcade, Charlotte pauses to watch a player with a toy guitar, another dancing to the beat pre-choreographed on the screen.

In the more tranquil spaces she visits, she moves. In Kyoto, she ascends the stairs to enter the Nanzen-ji temple. She passes a

couple en route to their marriage ceremony approaching the gate from the opposite side and pauses to watch as the groom tentatively takes the bride's hand. The red of the couple's umbrella matches the red of Charlotte's purse, subtly linking her to them. She navigates the stepping stones through a lily pond at the Heian-jingu shrine before tying a paper wish to a tree. As she exits, she traverses the vast courtyard of the shrine grounds, walking with purpose – as she will again at the film's end.

Sound and music are keys to mapping the cultural divide. In the hotel, we hear ambient noise (elevator doors, conversation, running water). What music we do hear is Western, be it the soothing classical track from the television or the piped-in pop that accompanies aqua aerobics at the pool. The band in the bar recycles American folk and soft rock. In contrast to the sonorous gongs associated with the temple, manufactured bell sounds intrude: the elevator dings, the telephone rings, the fire alarm blares.

The film score deliberately blurs the divide, sonically suggesting the shuttling between cultures the characters experience. Electronic music allowed music supervisor Brian Reitzell to create an ambient sound detached from identifiably Eastern or Western traditions, as in his collaborations with Roger J. Manning Jr that play as Charlotte explores the subway and the Shibuya district. He recruited Kevin Shields to create instrumental accompaniments that would evoke 'a sense of disassociation, of being in an unfamiliar, alienating world'.[55] In fact, the electronic music is almost exclusively affiliated with Charlotte. We first hear it in the opening, and it accompanies her as she physically explores Japan or experiments with its culture, as in trying ikebana (traditional flower arranging) or hanging cherry blossoms in her room. As the soundtrack to her seeking, the score emphasises a blending of cultures. Reitzell played drums with musical group Air, who contributed 'Alone in Kyoto', the song that plays as she travels to Kyoto by train and subsequently enters the Nanzen-ji temple space. It melds vocal harmonies with plucking strings, piano and guitar riffs with bells, electronic tones with recorded wave sounds, suggesting her immersion in Japanese culture, as well as the transition from the enclosed, manufactured spaces of the city and hotel to the natural landscape outside the temple.

Like the film score, the famous karaoke scene blends Japanese culture with Western music as it unites Bob and Charlotte. Fittingly, Charlotte, more immersed in Japan through her solo travels and an existing network of friends, initiates their joint excursion, their 'prison break'. She takes him to meet her friend Charlie (Fumihiro Hayashi), who propels the couple on an Odyssean journey through Tokyo's nightlife. To announce Charlotte's influence on Bob, The Chemical Brothers' 'The State We're In' begins the moment they leave her room, continuing as they encounter Charlie and his friends. The song's upbeat electronic rhythm, fused with flashes of light and animated chatter, captures the energy they find among the locals and with each other. Together, Bob and Charlotte not only move but *run* through Tokyo's streets. Fleeing an altercation between Charlie and a bartender armed with a BB gun, they dash into the street and dart into a noisy pachinko parlour, weaving through aisles of players sitting before screens, an amped-up version of Charlotte's desultory stroll through the arcade.

The evening ends at the karaoke bar. The sequence opens with Charlie singing The Sex Pistols' 'God Save the Queen', the very performance that inspired the film. It is a bravura sequence, a memorable climax that unites the film's themes, particularly those associated with Bob. Like the behind-the-scenes sequences, it self-reflexively highlights performance: the group don wigs to sing along to scripted music. Yet it has none of the distancing artifice of Bob's commercial work. These are amateurs, not professionals, willingly performing songs of their own choosing and for an audience of friends, not consumers. Charlie belts out the song, deliberately rolling his 'r's – like Johnny Rotten – but also in a seeming riposte to the stereotypical 'l–r' confusion. The lyrics to Bob's first song, '(What's So Funny 'Bout) Peace, Love and Understanding', echo the cross-cultural messaging, affirmed by reaction shots of the assembled

Japanese. Together, Charlie and Charlotte, wearing a bright pink wig, sing The Pretenders' 'Brass in Pocket', and for a moment she becomes the celebrity, though for an audience of one: Bob. Despite the presence of others, close-up reaction shots focus on the two: as Charlotte sings 'I'm special', Bob mouths 'special'. Charlotte takes the place of the talk show host to 'formally' introduce Bob – 'Ladies and Gentlemen, Mr Bob Harris' – before he begins an off-key rendition of Roxy Music's 'More Than This'.[56] Her mock announcement and his amateurish singing are both deliberate choices that skewer celebrity pretensions. By contrast, the lyrics – 'more than this / there's nothing more than this' – telegraph their inchoate feelings, underscored by close-up reaction shots of the two of them.

Ingeniously, the film's music flirts with generic expectations. Romantic comedies infamously substitute popular music lyrics in place of dialogue – the fifteen to twenty popular songs marketing ploy. Instead, except for snippets of songs played in context at parties and in clubs during the couple's nights out in Tokyo, and 'Just Like Honey', which plays over the final scene and credits, any popular music with identifiable lyrics is performed in the film's context – by its actors or the professional musicians in the Park Hyatt bar. The karaoke performances allow the film to have it both ways: the characters substitute lyrics for dialogue, verbally expressing feelings they do not articulate directly. Simultaneously, they enact the film's critique of celebrity: identifiable performers, particularly Bill Murray, engage in genuine, amateur singing. Together, these dimensions of their performances convey the authenticity of the connection they have forged through their immersion in Japanese culture. The point is made clear when they return to the hotel after another night on the town together and discover Kelly, the 'actress', earnestly singing 'Nobody Does it Better' on the bar's karaoke machine to an unresponsive audience of drunken strangers. The artifice of the scene – the hotel's American version of the Tokyo late-night staple, the exaggerated performance of a professional – stresses its inauthenticity. The karaoke scene also heightens the sting of Bob's dalliance with the 'red-haired singer' of Sausalito: he has chosen a professional performer rather than Charlotte, a fake over the real.[57]

Another iconic image from the film shows the transformation the couple's shared experiences of Tokyo have had on them. At the end of their karaoke performances, Charlotte takes a cigarette break in the hallway. Bob exits the booth to join her, traversing the hallway towards her. Given the significance of the hallway space in the hotel – as a public place of transition – it is striking to note the differences: unlike the open, seemingly endless halls of the hotel, this appears intimate and enclosed; rather than blandly decorated,

it features zebra-striped panels at sharp angles against blue walls. In combination with the orange flash of Bob's T-shirt and Charlotte's pink wig, the colours and patterns invoke those associated with Tokyo, with the talk show host's bold striped suit and pop-toned set, and Charlie's Hawaiian-style shirt. Bob wordlessly takes a drag from her cigarette (a visual retort to John's criticism of her smoking), before she rests her head on his shoulder, a gesture that prefigures his resting his hand on Charlotte's shoulder after returning to the hotel. At these moments of profound connection, no words are necessary.

Cabs and limousines, while moving vehicles like Tokyo's subways and trains, serve as amalgams of motion and stasis in the film, bridging divides between the US and Japan in airport transfer and between the hotel and Japanese sights. Fittingly, they link Bob and Charlotte, too. Returning from the karaoke bar to the Park Hyatt, Charlotte assumes the same position as Bob had when he first arrived in Tokyo, seated on the right side of a taxi cab's back seat, admiring the passing cityscape. As in the case of Bob's arrival, the lights reflect off the window that separates Charlotte from the city itself. It is a liminal space: the couple are stationary, but the vehicle moves. And, in this instance, the two share the space, Bob dozing on the seat beside her, in the same position he had occupied on the bench outside the karaoke booth. Later, returning by limousine from his

talk show appearance, Bob, seated on the right side of the back seat, slips from his pocket a Polaroid of Charlotte taken on their karaoke night. Their shared experiences of Tokyo have transformed their relationship – and each as individuals, especially Bob.

The scene in the limo shows him focused on the photo, not on the passing display as he had on his arrival in Japan, blinking and rubbing his eyes as though in disbelief at the sight of his own image on a billboard. At the time, he was disconnected from the city and himself. The alteration is pronounced when he sees the same image, though this time from the street and with Charlotte. After another night-time excursion, they again race through the busy streets – Charlotte wearing his jacket – dodging stationary cabs before spotting the Suntory advertisement on the side of a moving truck. 'There you are,' Charlotte points. 'Say hi.' Bob waves. In Tokyo and in her company, he (at least temporarily) puts his stardom in its place.

During their late-night conversation in bed, Charlotte says, 'Let's never come here again, because it would never be as much fun.' In a departure from the rest of the scene, the two are filmed reflected in the bedroom window, the lights of Tokyo forming a film over them – just as in the taxi windows. Words and image combine to remind us of the transitory nature of travel and the reality that both are merely passing through.

5 Departures

Eventually, and inevitably, trips end. Travellers leave – either to return home or to continue on their journeys. The time comes to say goodbye. *Lost in Translation* ends with two goodbyes – the final one we all remember and another one just before it that we might not.

They appear, in retrospect, dictated by the film's themes and structure. It follows two travellers, so it shows two departures, each in keeping with the characters' independent searches for purpose and self. The goodbye scenes reflect the film's bifurcated settings: the first occurs in the hotel, the second in Tokyo's streets.

The doubled goodbyes are prefigured by the fumbled goodnight kiss Bob and Charlotte share in the hotel elevator. As we've seen, the kiss occurs twice in the moving enclosure. Once, Bob tries to exit but fails after he misses his floor. Then Charlotte exits at her floor, while Bob stays on board to return to his.

The goodbyes reverse this pattern: Bob leaves the hotel and Tokyo, while Charlotte stays (at least temporarily). Bob's departure initially occurs in the hotel lobby, a public space that reinforces his celebrity status. The hotel staff and his Suntory handlers engage in formal, prolonged rituals of departure, wishing him a good flight, asking if he's had a good trip, etc. He retreats to use the hotel phone to call Charlotte, covering his disappointment when he gets her voicemail by leaving a jokey message:

Charlotte, I'm down in the lobby, and I'm leaving now. Um, I was calling to see if you still have my jacket ... if you could bring it down, but you're not there, so this is goodbye, and, uh ... So, I guess, goodbye and enjoy my jacket which you stole from me.

Just like their fumbled kiss, the goodbye eventually lands: Charlotte was descending the elevator with his jacket as he called.

The jacket is not incidental – the prop for his joke or excuse for his call. Charlotte borrowed it the night they wove through parked cars and spotted Bob's larger-than-life image on the rolling billboard, when he, through her eyes, acknowledged his stardom with wonder rather than regret. She returns his jacket against a similar backdrop. As Charlotte appears, Bob has been accosted by an attractive female fan who has furtively waited to approach him. While he can extricate himself from her flirtatious attentions, he cannot shake his 'bodyguards', as he calls the Suntory representatives, so their parting words are cursory. Even Charlotte cringes at his lame attempt at humour: 'Aren't you going to wish me "have a good fright" or something?' Their parting words are banal in the extreme: 'Well, bye,' Charlotte says. 'All right,' Bob responds.

We can see, however, that, as in the elevator, they want to embrace, but in this case their discomfort at being in a public space makes it impossible. They had initially met in the elevator, exchanging glances. Their hotel goodbye reverses the scene. Bob, enlisted to take one more picture with the Suntory team, alternates his gaze between posing for the camera and watching Charlotte depart. A close-up on his face registers the stark distinction between 'Bob Harris', the actor

who smiles wanly for his snapshot, and Bob, the man who looks
dolefully in Charlotte's direction. As the elevator door chimes, we
adopt his point of view to see Charlotte enter through the opening
doors and turn to look briefly in his direction before the mirrored
doors close, substituting the reflected image of a bowing bellman in
her stead. While we have heard the doors chime and open and close,
this is our first – and last – view of the elevator's exterior. We are no
longer with the couple finding each other inside it. We are outside.
Like Bob, we have lost Charlotte.

Until, that is, he finally leaves the hotel. The scene of their
second and final goodbye is memorable, for it conforms, not to
generic expectations, but those established by the film itself – and on
so many levels. We do not hear the words we expect them to share,
the ones they would have exchanged in a less public space. They
are, of course, surrounded, as in the hotel lobby, by others. And, as
viewers, we occupy the same position as onlookers, no different than
the prying fans or curious strangers. However, that is not the reason
for the film's reticence. As we have seen, the couple communicates
only through sparky humour, or, at moments of greatest intimacy,
with few to no words at all. The characters who do speak are
superficial and vapid. Coppola relies instead on audiovisual means to
imaginatively engage us with the characters and fill in the gaps. We do
not simply hear the elevator and watch Charlotte leave; we feel Bob's
loss. The emotional impact of his rediscovery of her is even more
potent. Image and music fuse to engage us as dialogue would not.

A close-up of Bob's hand as he cradles her head shuttles us back
to three moments: when he rests his hand on her shoulder and later
on her foot in bed, and when they hold hands in the bar (a gesture
itself redolent with meaning for it evokes the scene of the bride
and groom holding hands at the temple). We see them kiss without
hesitation or fumbling. A familiar pattern of cutting between the
two draws them closer to each other even as they separate, with Bob
walking backwards to hold her gaze for as long as possible. Both
smile, and the single word they exchange – 'okay' – is affirmative

(and repeated for emphasis), suggesting that they have each found some sort of resolution.

Of course, this resolution is unlike those in the other films to which *Lost in Translation* has been compared. In *Brief Encounter*, for example, we hear Alec (Trevor Howard) and Laura (Celia Johnson) declare their feelings and vow to return to their respective spouses – and to remember each other. It closes definitively by revealing that the film we have been watching has been Laura's memory, unfurling (via voiceover) from her living room. 'You've been a long way away,' her husband (Cyril Raymond) says. 'Thank you for coming back to me.' Laura, at least, is no longer lost in thoughts of the past, but returned to her marriage in the present. (We can only assume that Alec has departed for Africa as planned.) By contrast, the couple in Richard Linklater's *Before Sunrise* (1995), who also depart on separate trains, commit to do the opposite: they will meet again exactly six months from their first encounter. We are equally sure of their feelings for each other, for they speak incessantly about their attitudes to romance before parting. The closest parallel may be Wong Kar-wai's *In the Mood for Love* (2000), which concludes with a scene of Chow Mo-wan (Tony Leung) at Angkor Wat speaking his secret, his thwarted love for Su Lizhen (Maggie Cheung), into a hole in the temple wall before sealing it with mud. However, title cards at the end summarise them for us: 'He remembers those vanished years. As though looking through a dusty windowpane, the past is something he could see, but not touch. And everything he sees is blurred and indistinct.'

Instead, Coppola's film ends, as we should have expected, with the originality and subtlety characteristic of the rest of the film. It feels right. Bob's backward walk physically represents his return home, as though the film is running backwards towards the start. He returns to the waiting taxi to retrace his route back to the airport to fly home, presumably in time to attend his daughter's dance recital (as Lydia had reminded him by phone). He will, it appears, resume his established life and career. At the moment Charlotte made him say 'hi' to his celebrity image rolling down the Tokyo street, he appeared to make peace with his identity. His actor persona is a part he assumes but it does not define him. He also has another role to play in life, as a husband and father. Although never visible on screen, Lydia was continually present in the film through messages and calls focused on his obligations. Bob's return to his family suggests the simultaneous end of his midlife and marital crises.

By contrast, John, who was initially present, has been absent for the final two-thirds of the film – off screen while working elsewhere on a shoot. We see one faxed message from him – a drawing of a heart announcing his return – but no evidence that Charlotte did. It arrives as she must have been descending the elevator to say goodbye to Bob. As they part in the street, she walks away from Bob in the opposite direction, away from the hotel and, we infer, from home. She does not leave. She stays, swallowed up by the crowd, as though enfolded by a new culture and experience. She walks towards the camera and then out of the film frame and the film itself, a sign of her independence. It seems she has found the opposite solution to her crisis: she will not return to her marriage. She will continue her search for meaning and purpose on her own – without John or Bob. He had told her, 'You'll figure that out. I'm not worried about you.'

If we accept, as Coppola suggested, that Bob and Charlotte occupy ends of the same continuum, their separate trajectories at the film's conclusion seem inevitable: they have each been transformed *by* the other, not *for* the other. The ending avoids the clichéd conclusions to romantic films, too. Bob doesn't resolve his midlife/ marital crisis by finding a younger partner. Nor does Charlotte find the solution to her existential crisis – who is she? what is she going to do or be? – in a relationship with another, older man. Instead, Bob revises his view of himself through her eyes and she does the same through his. They part, changed by having been together, to resume their evolving paths, travelling separately but in the same direction: forwards in time, yet from different points – hers nearer the start, his nearer the end – each carrying memories of the time spent in each other's company.

Musical cues accompany and guide visual interpretation. For the first time, a non-diegetic popular song with lyrics plays over the images. Until the goodbye scene, the soundtrack has incorporated ambient sounds or electronic-based music. When popular songs have appeared, they occurred in the context of performance – during karaoke, at parties and nightclubs, in the Park Hyatt bar. As Bob releases Charlotte and begins walking away, we hear drumming and then the initial beats of 'Just Like Honey'.[58] When the film cuts to

Charlotte, The Jesus and Mary Chain's lyrics begin playing as she walks into the crowd:

> Listen to the girl
> As she takes on half the world
> Moving up and so alive
> In her honey dripping beehive[59]

They reinforce the visual image: we watch Charlotte from behind, her honey-blonde hair cascading down her back, as she embraces a new path forward. When the film cuts to Bob re-entering the cab, we hear the continuation, beginning with the repetition of 'beehive', a subtle sonic parallel to the thematic doubling.

As they continue, the lyrics echo their final affirmations – 'so good', 'all right' (the words Bob uses to the driver as a signal to go) – and imply the effort it took Bob to leave: it was a hard thing to do. (Clearly, he's walking away from her not 'to' her as in the song, but we still get the point.) The male and female vocalists (Jim Reid and Karen Parker) harmonise on 'just like honey' as point-of-view shots from inside the limo show the passing cityscape. The couple's brief sojourn in Tokyo was 'just like honey': sweet. The phrase repeats over the credits, prolonging the sensation for viewers – within the film space and beyond.

Two additional songs, played over the credits and uncoupled from images, similarly extend the film narrative. One is a Western track, the other Japanese, befitting its fusion of cultures. The first, 'City Girl', was one of four songs Kevin Shields composed expressly for the film.[60] His vocals speak for Bob about 'city girl' Charlotte, who is 'free to learn' and 'free to go':

> I wanted you
> I do
> I do
> I do ...

I love you
I do
I do
I do[61]

The lyrics supply the dialogue denied us in their final embrace while equating Charlotte with Tokyo as the 'city girl'.

In a sense, the final song supplies the 'happy ending' we hoped for: 'Kaze wo Atsumete', an acoustic folk song by pioneering Japanese rock musicians Happy End. It leaves us with Charlotte, for the lyrics offer a wanderer's fantastical, romanticised descriptions of the Tokyo cityscape.[62] Originally released in the 1960s, the song associates the ethereal city with the past, as though it is already a memory.

The songs are aural snapshots, audio equivalents of the cinematographic images pieced together, collage-style, that constitute the film. As Coppola would later say in interviews, 'The film is a memory of something that only lasts a short time yet stays with you for ever.' While she was referring to the narrative, the idea that Bob and Charlotte will remember their brief encounter, her words apply as well to how the film lingers in our minds. It so thoroughly immerses us in a virtual audiovisual experience lasting only 102 minutes that long afterwards we can recall the images we have seen, the music we have heard – and that we did *not* hear Bob's final words to Charlotte. By denying them, the film makes us reflect on our desire to know. Like voyeurs, we have gained access to their bedrooms and conversations, and feel entitled to know their feelings. We have grown accustomed to genre fiction (literature as well as film) providing us with the satisfying resolution we seek. By withholding Bob's words, the film suggests we really shouldn't have expected to know – not only in a moral sense, as in it's none of our business, but existentially.[63] Definite answers and complete closure are the stuff of fiction, not life. Paradoxically, the film – like the photoshoot, the commercial, the television show – is a work of fiction, yet it conveys an essential truth about human relationships: it is an illusion that we can ever gain access to a couple's intimate lives.

As an artwork, *Lost in Translation* relies on cinema's synthesis of sound, image and motion to convey meaning. Because it invites, even requires, such active participation, the film has an enduring power – in our individual memories and in cinematic history.

6 Reception

Lost in Translation evocatively represents the bifurcated nature of travel as an amalgam of stasis and motion. Travellers leave and return by plane, streaking through the atmosphere at great speed across time zones while sensing themselves at rest, often interminably so. As we have seen, the film employs other forms of conveyance – elevators, cars, subways, trains – that shuttle travellers from one space to another as they retain a sense of stillness, paradoxically reinforced by the scenes passing by glimpsed through windows. These act as the film frame, reminding attentive audiences of their own position as unmoving spectators watching moving images – or, in fact, images that are still and only appear to move. The characters move, the city moves, the film moves – and moves us.

To do so, the film itself travelled – first in sections transported to editor Sarah Flack in the US, and then, once assembled, on the festival circuit – to Telluride, Venice and Toronto – before returning for its official release in the US. At each stop, the film was warmly received. In her memoir *Notes on a Life*, Eleanor Coppola recalls being with her husband in Belize and receiving daily phone calls and emails from Sofia:

'Mom, we heard we're getting a good review from the *New York Times*!' Francis calls out from his computer, 'The *Wall Street Journal* gave it a terrific review.' An email from the West Coast says, 'Did you know the SF [*San Francisco*] *Chronicle* gave it a little man clapping, falling out of his chair! It's the best you can get.' 'Ebert and Roper gave it two thumbs up!'[64]

Major American critics declared it one of the year's best films. 'An insouciant triumph' came the word from the UK.[65] Coppola was acknowledged as a director with an original vision.

She 'communicates so clearly in a cinematic language all her own', Lisa Schwarzbaum wrote for *Entertainment Weekly*.[66] 'She boasts one of today's truly distinct filmmaking voices,' said another critic.[67] The film's complex balance of drama and comedy was variously attributed to Coppola's writing and Murray's acting. The film is 'fraught with a deep sadness and sense of yearning', yet also 'enormously' funny, 'not because it feels any obligation to be "funny" in some contrived, screenwriterly sort of way, but because Coppola has set out to make a movie set to the rhythms of real (rather than reel) life', Scott Foundas wrote, recognising the film's commitment to authenticity.[68] To Kenneth Turan, 'The fact that this kind of serious material ends up playing puckishly funny as well as poignant is a tribute both to Coppola and to her do-or-die decision to cast Murray in the lead role.'[69] This is the Bill Murray performance 'we've been waiting for: *Saturday Night Live* meets Chekhov'.[70] David Ansen and others contended that Scarlett Johansson was his match. 'If Murray has an imposing corner on the comic dynamism in this movie, Johansson is no less compelling for her mysticism, self-assurance and charm,' Desson Howe argued. 'She's as vital to this movie as he is.'[71]

Critics also recognised the vital contributions of cinematography, editing, sound and music to the film. Acord was praised for his 'loose, agile camerawork' and 'eagle eye for cultural absurdities'.[72] He 'makes Tokyo a gaudy dreamscape', and, as Peter Rainer eloquently put it, registers the perspective of its lost travellers:

the movie, which was shot by Lance Acord in lustrous nocturnal tones, presents Japan as an outsider might see it, without apology. The night-worlds both within the hotel and without are equally odd and forbidding. Everything seems hushed – suspended in time – and yet there is always the sense of violence about to break loose. In Japan, the most extreme delicacy goes hand in hand with garishness, and Coppola offers up both for our delectation. It's a heady, hallucinatory combo.[73]

Several critics identified Brian Reitzell's hand in the score, likening his contributions to *Lost in Translation* to his previous work on *The Virgin Suicides*, which was, as Elvis Mitchell described, 'informed more substantially by the score ... than by the narrative'. Mitchell also recognised that sound in *Lost in Translation* worked in concert with music: 'Sound is used so beautifully it takes your breath away; in a scene where Bob carries the dozing Charlotte to her room, the hotel corridor is gently dusted with aural density; the noise of air conditioners and fluorescent lights becomes a part of the milieu.'[74] He identifies a scene Coppola herself singled out for praise. She marvelled at how sound designer Richard Beggs carried over the Bloody Valentine song Reitzell selected for the cab ride, muffling it for the hallway scene.[75]

But it was the ending that captured many critics' hearts, presaging its enduring influence on viewers. Calling it 'a moment of intimate magnificence', *Salon* critic Stephanie Zacharek wrote, 'I have never seen anything quite like it, in any movie.'[76] Richard Corliss recognised the two-part structure that grants the final scene its emotional power. Writing for *Time* magazine, he advised viewers, 'Watch Murray's eyes in the climactic scene in the hotel lobby: while hardly moving, they express the collapsing of all hopes, the return to a sleepwalking status quo.'[77]

Several cited the impact of the final goodbye. Roger Ebert unabashedly confessed, 'I loved the moment near the end when Bob runs after Charlotte and says something in her ear, and we're not allowed to hear it.'[78] To at least one reviewer, critics and audiences were not the only ones moved: 'It gets at something exquisitely human, so human even movie stars feel it.'[79]

Despite these accolades, the film had – and continues to have – its share of detractors. *The New Yorker*'s David Denby called Coppola 'two thirds of a great director':

the movie could use something grander, fiercer – danger, perhaps. It takes a great deal of courage for a young director to make a movie without action; it takes even greater courage to allow something momentous to happen. Coppola already knows many of the secrets of character, atmosphere, and comedy. Now she has to learn that she can shape a movie dramatically without slipping into banality or vulgarity.[80]

The 'vulgarity' he notes refers, of course, to the controversial presentation of Japanese people. Though he praised the film and Bill Murray's performance in particular, David Edelstein also had reservations:

There's something a little narcissistic and entitled about these two people that isn't a great advertisement for Americans abroad. Charlotte asks Bob why the Japanese mix up their L's and R's, and he says, 'For yucks,' which is a very funny line, pure Bill Murray. But there are yucks, at their expense. The sense of otherness and of cultural superiority merges uncomfortably.[81]

In *TV Guide*, Ken Fox was more blunt:

Coppola shows us Japan solely through the eyes of her characters, who see the Japanese as cartoonishly infantile, infatuated with asinine TV shows, karaoke and silly video games. It can be funny, but the humor is too often based in stereotypical perceptions of Asians (they're short, they're laughably polite, they eat weird food), and Coppola shamelessly invites us to laugh along with Murray's character.[82]

Fox's comment, however, contains an important observation: the view of the Japanese comes from the characters, especially – if not exclusively – Bob, rather than the film as a whole.

Richard Corliss identified it as 'America's cultural myopia at work abroad'.[83] The degree to which the film holds up its characters' cultural myopia for critique has preoccupied critics and scholars ever since. Fifteen years later, Mairead Small Staid agreed with Corliss: 'In each of his interactions – whether with director and photographer or with a shower head, an exercise machine – the joke's on him. He is the stereotype, the caricature, sketched in only the faintest strokes.'[84]

Two decades on, Bob's ugly-American-cluelessness has been thrown into higher relief, not only because of heightened sensitivity to cultural stereotyping (especially given the rise of anti-Asian violence in the wake of the COVID-19 pandemic) but because Japanese culture has become embedded in Western culture. Karaoke nights are ubiquitous in cities large and small, and Americans drink Japanese whisky – Suntory as well as Nikka, Yamazaki, Hibiki and other brands. Bob could now easily substitute Japanese food for 'all that pasta', as he tells his wife he wants to when he returns. Her retort – 'why don't you just stay there and you can have it every day?' – is still cutting but now also comic since sushi bars and ramen shops are as common as taco stands and hamburger joints, and hot-pot (*shabu shabu*) restaurants are trending. As a result, the film's satire is more evident and even more biting.

At the time of the film's release, critic Carrie Rickey noted that focusing on the 'condescending jokes' in scenes involving Bob is itself myopic. She wrote,

More representative of the movie's tone is a sequence in which Charlotte, wandering through the hotel meeting rooms, exits a shrill news conference for an American action movie and enters a room where women serenely practice the art of ikebana, traditional flower arranging. Coppola makes the contrast between the hyperbole of American commercialism and the harmony of Japanese art as lyrical as a haiku.[85]

Writing for the British magazine *Sight & Sound*, Paul Julian Smith agreed. He claimed, 'In fact the cruellest and crudest satire is against Los Angeles,'[86] a point that continues to resonate given the ongoing Hollywoodisation of global entertainment culture.

Others pointed to Coppola's personal connection to Japan, her casting of Japanese friends and real-life hotel employees, as well as the Japanese members of the crew, including assistant director Takahide Kawakami. However, in *Cineaste*, Maria San Filippo noted that even though 'the film is largely credited by Japanese crewmembers … no sympathetic or even fleshed-out Japanese character is portrayed on screen'. She attributes this 'retreat into America-centrism' to the director's commitment to authenticity, describing it as 'truthful' to travel and to the travel film:

Claiming that her portrayal is based on her own travel experience, Coppola knows firsthand that American tourists rarely get to know any Japanese well enough to discover their depth as sympathetic human beings. It is ignorance tempered by a well-honed human instinct to avoid stepping out of one's comfort zone – in travel as in relationships, is the implication. Moreover, the travelers' tale, like its homegrown cousin the road movie, relies on a paradoxical immersion within the unfamiliar – at a distance.[87]

Frank Tomasula sees allusions to Wim Wenders' *Tokyo-Ga* (1985) and Chris Marker's *Sans soleil* (1983), 'visual essays that [similarly] depict Westerners lost in Tokyo'.[88]

Film scholar Homay King finds no resolution, arguing that the film does not 'sufficiently clarify' its point of view: 'When Japan appears superficial, inappropriately erotic, or unintelligible, we are never completely sure whether this vision belongs to Coppola, to her characters, or simply to a Hollywood cinematic imaginary that has been offering up such images of the East at least since Cecil B. DeMille's 1915 *The Cheat*.' As a result, she argues that at no point does the film securely occupy a position of condescension and stresses its attempts to represent the experience of being lost:

Sensations of incomprehension, of loss of control, of forgetting even the time of day, tend to dominate. These sensations, the film makes clear, can be highly pleasurable, and even transformative when one is open to them … Cityscapes that appear to defy the laws of Western perspective, curving off-ramps that seem to defy gravity – these are rendered all the more exhilarating because Bob and Charlotte cannot read them, and thus may appreciate them for their visual properties. Such images revel in the feeling of lostness without attempting to muffle its shock with cheap humor.[89]

This sense of being lost is, as we have seen, the film's central focus. *Lost in Translation* is composed, as Alice Lovejoy observed in *Film Comment*, of 'isolated points that crystallise the traveler's narrative of transience. Delirious with exhaustion, set apart by language, culture, ethnicity, and time zone, the film's characters sense themselves in relief against the world around them.'[90]

The 'cheap humor' of Bob's scenes does stand out, as the object of the film's critique and the audience's, then and now, an era even more keenly attentive to anti-Asian bias. However, to claim the entire film is an 'insufferable, racist mess' or charge Coppola with 'aesthetic racism' fails to consider the film's nuances and ambiguities.[91] As Lucy Bolton points out, Bob's jokes are intended to make Charlotte laugh, but she 'does not generally go along with this type of humor'.[92] His humour, though, is equally a sign, as we've seen, of his dissociation from his celebrity image, from the tired construct of masculine stardom the Japanese scripts perpetuate. Bolton also cautions against taking the film's depiction of Tokyo and the Japanese as 'one note', citing the couple's explorations of the city in each other's company and in the company of Japanese friends. In such scenes, as Todd McGowan and Sharon Lin Tay have argued, the film actually *reverses* other stereotypical cinematic tropes. McGowan notes that the American characters do not uncover 'a mysterious essence at the heart of Japanese society' that sparks a self-transformation. Tay contends they are not like characters 'in imperialistic narratives about (male) explorers and bounty hunters going out to explore, exploit, and take possession of the Orient'.[93] They are not, in other words, like the actress Kelly, whom the film mocks for her cultural appropriations of Buddhism and karate. Such complications – distinctions among characters, differences of point of view, alterations in tone, generic influences – to say nothing of the complex role of music in relation to film image, work against simplistic dismissals of the film or its director as racist.

Without question, however, there were anxieties about how the film would play in Japan. The film's Japanese distributor delayed its opening, restricting screening to one Tokyo cinema. Local reviews reflected the same divided opinion found in reviews abroad. Yoshio Tsuchiya described it as 'stereotypical and discriminatory'.[94] Yet, another found its presentation of Tokyo the opposite: 'The film is not taken through the eyes of tourists or Japan maniacs who assume they know the culture very well; Tokyo is rather an unknown and foreign planet, filled with fragile beauty.' Yasuhisa Harada, anticipating film scholars, directed attention to context and character: 'In the United States, some people were concerned that the film might appear as anti-Japanese. Despite that fact, the film neither tries to dissolute Tokyo nor investigates it; the peculiarity and wonder of the city is accurately reflected. Tokyo was simply picked as the setting for Murray's lonely, wandering self who is at the brink of losing his entire perception on life.'[95]

As Harada noted, some in the US did have concerns about representation: on 31 January 2004, the Los Angeles-based organisation Asia Mediawatch launched a campaign against the film's four Academy Award nominations.[96] At least one scholar has faulted the campaign for assuming 'that the "Japanese" are a generic category who should be presented in a particular way', and questioned the group's focus on Coppola's film. 'What was most strange about the controversy over *Lost in Translation*, however, was why this film should have aroused such passion when it appeared at the same time as *The Last Samurai*, a film whose portrayal of Japan was objectively far more suspect.'[97]

Nevertheless, the campaign had little influence on Academy voters. The film did lose the Oscar for Best Picture, which went to Peter Jackson for *The Lord of the Rings: The Return of the King*, but Coppola won for Best Original Screenplay. The 2004 award season brought additional accolades, many noteworthy for a female director in a male-dominated industry: Coppola's three nominations at the Academy Awards made her the first American woman to be nominated for directing (and only the third female director in its history at the time). She was the first woman to be Oscar-nominated for writing, directing and producing in the same year. Her nomination for the Screen Directors Guild made her only the fifth woman to be nominated in its history. As Eleanor wrote, there had been 'no woman in a decade'.[98]

And though the film lost at the Oscars, it won at the Golden Globes, Independent Spirit and AFI award ceremonies – and garnered nominations for its crew across all major categories (cinematography, editing, production design, sound, music and acting). No one earned more awards than Bill Murray. Writing for *Rolling Stone*, Peter Travers had predicted 'Bill Murray and Scarlett Johansson give performances that will be talked about for years'.[99] He was right.

The film transformed both actors' careers. Johansson, who had been acting since she was a young child, had only appeared in a handful of features. Coppola had admired her performance in *Manny & Lo* (1996) when the actress was only eleven: 'She had that husky voice even then and seemed mature beyond her years. There was some quality about her that stood out and I connected with. She's able to convey a lot without saying anything.'[100] Coppola felt that the seventeen-year-old Johansson (she turned eighteen during the shoot) could play a character in her early twenties. Her turn as Charlotte marked her transition to adult roles, especially when paired with her performance in *Girl with a Pearl Earring* (2003), which was released the same year. Johansson was nominated for Golden Globe awards for both films, and won the BAFTA for Best Actress for *Lost in Translation*. After appearing in several Woody Allen films, she shot to global stardom as Black Widow in the Marvel blockbusters (eight times and counting). How ironic, given that she appeared in *Lost in Translation* as the inverse of Kelly, the airheaded actress promoting her role as an action-film star. Two films appearing in 2019 – *Marriage Story* and *Jojo Rabbit* – earned her a second set of nominations, this time for two Oscars (Best Actress and Best Supporting Actress). In both films, she plays characters who might be described as grown-up versions of Charlotte: a woman going through a divorce in *Marriage Story* and a single mother in *Jojo Rabbit*. One writer for *The Cut* magazine connected the dots from *Lost in Translation* to *Marriage Story* in particular, pinpointing 'the curious through line of Scarlett Johansson's career: She is a frequent vessel for divorce'.[101]

Murray, like his character, came to the film with an already established reputation as an ironic, smart-alecky comedian, having starred on *SNL* and in films such as *Caddyshack* (1980) and *Ghostbusters* (1984). He had also achieved a sort of 'secular sainthood' based on his off-screen antics, such as random appearances at bars, restaurants and even construction sites, and for side-stepping Hollywood protocols, like having an agent, in favour of the 800-number Coppola used to leave messages for him.[102] She did not think of Bill Murray as Bob Harris but Bob Harris as Bill Murray. Elvis Mitchell got that: 'He plays a vodka-and-bitters version of himself and the persona that made him famous.'[103] Still, Coppola's film transformed Murray. His potential for drama had been evident in *Groundhog Day* (1993) and *Rushmore*, a performance Coppola said she'd liked. But, as the effusive reviews attested, this was

Murray unlike we had ever seen him before. After completing the film, Murray said it was his favourite performance.[104] It clearly holds a place in others' memories. In 2020, seventeen years after the film's release, author Roddy Doyle was asked, 'Whom would you want to write your life story?' He answered, 'I haven't a clue. But if there's a movie based on the book, I'd like Bill Murray's facial expression in "Lost in Translation" to play me. Not Bill – just his facial expression.'[105] When Coppola and Murray reunited for *On the Rocks*, critics inevitably (and perhaps unfairly) judged the older actor in relation to his past self. Manohla Dargis's take sounds eerily like Elvis Mitchell's: 'Murray wears his roles lightly, so you always feel that you're getting some version of the actor himself, the comic legend (funny, dry, unknowable).'[106]

Like Bill Murray's expression, the film's music attracted a devoted following of its own. While Reitzell and Shields were nominated for a BAFTA award for Best Film Music, the album garnered praise beyond the film industry. Years later Frank Mojica called the soundtrack the 'third star of the picture', and credited the film with reviving 'shoegaze' music, noting that both My Bloody Valentine and The Jesus and Mary Chain regrouped in the 2000s. (Scarlett Johansson sang along to 'Just Like Honey' when The Jesus and Mary Chain performed at Coachella in 2007.)[107] The soundtrack has been featured as one of the best of all time on lists published by *Rolling Stone* and *Pitchfork*.[108]

The phenomenal success of *Lost in Translation* paved the way for Coppola to direct her first (and possibly only) film for a big studio, *Marie Antoinette*, with a budget ten times the size of *Lost in Translation*'s. After completing *The Virgin Suicides*, she had intended to adapt Antonia Fraser's biography of Marie Antoinette but was dissatisfied with her script and put it aside, writing *Lost in Translation* quickly 'as a little project to do while she gave herself time'.[109] Superficially, the two films appear worlds apart: one is a spare, low-budget production about two jet-lagged travellers set in contemporary Japan, the other a lavish biopic about an infamous historical personage set in eighteenth-century France. However, scholars have since linked the director's first three films as a 'trilogy' on young women's rites of passage from adolescence to adulthood, and the case could be made for tracing versions of Charlotte through the other films in Coppola's canon. To some degree, most feature female characters searching for identity and purpose, often in opposition to repressive social forces manifested on screen as enclosed spaces, from bedrooms to palaces and plantations. Even in *On the Rocks*, Laura perceives herself trapped in her New York apartment by domestic duties. It's worth recalling that Rashida Jones, who plays Laura, originally workshopped the role of Charlotte, for in some senses she stands at the end of an evolving continuum, with the Lisbon sisters and the younger girls of *The Bling Ring* and *The Beguiled* at one end and the women who have married and had children at the other (not only Laura but Marie Antoinette, whom we follow as she travels the continuum's length from girlhood to imminent death). Charlotte occupies the middle: newly married, childless and possibly soon to divorce.

Yet just as *Lost in Translation* entwines Charlotte and Bob, a parallel continuum courses through Coppola's films focused on male experience. The story of the Lisbon sisters is the boys' story. Just as they narrate Eugenides' novel on which the film was based, theirs is the point of view from which we watch the girls. They are the ones, decades after the girls' suicides, still seeking to comprehend the events and uncouple themselves from their adolescent selves. As they say, 'The only way we could feel close to the girls was through these impossible excursions which have scarred us for ever, making us happier with dreams than wives.'

More intriguing is the thread that follows Bob. Coppola has described Murray as her muse and, in a sense, not simply for *Lost in Translation*. *Somewhere*, the feature that followed *Marie Antoinette*, is a reaction against that film's opulence and a return to the minimalism of *Lost in Translation*. Coppola toyed with making *Marie Antoinette* a silent film; she nearly succeeds in *Somewhere*, with a script even shorter than *Lost in Translation*'s. Johnny Marco (Stephen Dorff) is a younger version of Bob Harris: a male action star at the apex of his career, promoting his version of *Sunset Odds*, though disenchanted with his profession and, more to the point, his life. He is not reduced to Japandering,[110] but the film presents the tedium of promotion and performance in strikingly similar ways: like Bob, he occupies a temporary space, a room at the Chateau Marmont in Los Angeles. Johnny is also distant from his family – from his wife, from whom he has separated, and his daughter through his work-related absences.

He doesn't have Bob's midlife crisis Porsche; instead, he has a black Ferrari he drives in circles in the California desert, a metaphor for his own existential crisis, his own sense of being stuck. He is literally going nowhere. In a call that resembles Charlotte's to her friend Lauren, he confesses that he is 'nothing', 'not even a person'. As in Bob's case, he needs someone to 'find' him, to recognise him for himself, not as a celebrity, and propel him 'somewhere'. His Charlotte is also not a romantic partner – one-night stands and twin strippers fail to satisfy him. (They do not offer 'Premium Fantasy' but uninspired pole dances.) Johnny's catalyst for change arrives in the guise of his daughter, Cleo (Elle Fanning), as though Bob's daughter Zoe has grown up a bit and wandered into this film. Just as Bob presumably makes it home in time for his daughter's dance recital,

Somewhere (2010)

Johnny watches Cleo perform her ice-skating routine. However, like Charlotte, Cleo is Johnny's companion on excursions outside the hotel, including on a trip to Italy where he receives an award during a ceremony he cannot understand and where they stay in a suite at a hotel even more lavish than the Park Hyatt. As in *Lost in Translation*, an amateur performance unites them: Cleo rests her head on Johnny's shoulder in the lounge of the Chateau Marmont listening to waiter Romulo Laki serenade them with 'Teddy Bear'. A sign that Johnny has been transformed by their brief encounter is that he finally *moves* – out of the hotel and down the road.

Bill Murray, rather than an actor-surrogate like Dorff, reappears in *On the Rocks*, as Felix Keane. Even though Felix is not an actor, he is a quasi-celebrity, a successful gallery owner who performs for the waitresses who serve him (and even sings for patrons in a bar at a Mexican resort). He is a star in his own mind and in the screwball-comedy caper he concocts for himself and his daughter Laura (named after the song from the 1944 Otto Preminger film). Laura is an amalgam of Charlotte and Cleo: she is Felix's daughter but also becomes his dining and travel companion, as he usurps the place temporarily vacated by her husband Dean (Damon Wayans). She's the one who is stuck, though, blocked in her writing and fearing she has lost her husband – and the allure she once held for him. The ending is at once a repetition and reversal of *Lost in Translation*'s: Laura stays, yet at home, rather than in some exotic locale, and Felix leaves, departing not for home but for a cruise on the *Queen Mary*. She has become unstuck nevertheless, able to write again, and sees home and marriage, though unchanged, as if through the eyes of a traveller. In other words, she has arrived where she started and knows 'the place for the first time', as T. S. Eliot put it (though her 'travel' consists largely of one madcap ride through Manhattan and a quick hop to Mexico).[111]

Murray also played himself in *A Very Murray Christmas* (2015), a parody of the celebrity Christmas special Coppola directed for broadcast on Netflix. Visual references to *Lost in Translation* abound:

A Very Murray
Christmas (2015)

the film opens on a shot of Murray, forlornly surveying a cityscape
through the windows of his suite at the Carlyle hotel in New York.
He is a blend of Charlotte and Bob: like Charlotte he is framed
by the windows to dramatise his separation from the city (in this
case, by a snowstorm); like Bob he sports the male-star uniform: a
tuxedo (though jacket- and tie-less, accessorised by a pair of reindeer
antlers). As in *Lost in Translation*, we are granted behind-the-scenes
access to the rigours of performance, though here played for laughs
– with viewers in on the joke. Murray plays a version of himself
as the celebrity host of a fictional star-studded gala, a production
imperilled by the snowstorm that has prevented the performers and
guests from attending. As in *Lost in Translation*, the public spaces of
the hotel become the sets for 'improvised' performances. Stars play
themselves: Chris Rock joins Murray for a carol in the Café Carlyle
supper club, accompanied by Paul Shaffer on piano, a performance
as amateurish as Bob's karaoke. Musicians play characters as they
sing in Bemelmans Bar: Jenny Lewis is a waitress, the members of
the band Phoenix chefs. Other celebrities (Miley Cyrus and George
Clooney) appear in a dream version of the show that plays out in
Murray's head. He awakens, like Dorothy in *The Wizard of Oz*, to
discover himself back in his hotel room. He looks out once again
over the New York skyline, seeing it – as Laura does – with fresh
eyes, having travelled nowhere but in his imagination. (Or so the

film teases. Clooney exposes the fantasy as a fantasy: it was filmed 'on a soundstage in Queens'.)

Retrospectively, we can also see in Coppola's sophomore feature all the touchstones of the distinctive audiovisual style that has been branded 'Coppolism'. The natural lighting necessitated by their guerrilla-style methods in Japan has carried over into the softness characteristic of all her subsequent films, especially those shot, like *Lost in Translation*, on film to enhance their desaturated look. The muted colour palette associated with Charlotte is echoed in the dusky interiors and faded calico dresses of *The Beguiled*. However, it is evident even in *Marie Antoinette*, with its pastel palette modelled on Ladurée macarons, and *The Bling Ring*, with its suburban McMansions in washed-out pink. The minimal use of dialogue and slow pacing, which, in combination, establish the film's reflective mood, reach their peak in *Somewhere*, but the same strategy appears in all her films, even if only in moments, to grant heightened attention to interior states of anomie or alienation – the same psychological conditions experienced by Coppola's travellers (and the Lisbon sisters before them). Perhaps, above all, the painterly effect of static shots and imperceptible camera movements call our attention to *mise en scène*, to the placement of people and objects in the frame. The clutter of Charlotte's hotel room links her space to the ornamented rooms of the palace, plantation house and Paris Hilton's mansion.

The Bling Ring (2013)

Wide exterior shots reverberate: Kyoto courtyards and steps find their echo in scenes of the terraces and steps at Versailles; the electrified displays of Tokyo at night glimpsed from moving cars or through the hotel bar windows recur in street scenes in New York in *On the Rocks* and in Harris Savides' bravura shot in *The Bling Ring* of Audrina Patridge's hilltop glass house surrounded by the twinkling lights of LA. The window, ever representing the film frame, recurs as an insistent metaphor in the overarching theme uniting all Coppola films: seeing and being seen. Charlotte surveys Tokyo from her windowsill, Bob from his taxi. Edwina (Kirsten Dunst) peers down at Corporal McBurney (Colin Farrell) in *The Beguiled*. He looks up to see her watching, as we look up at Laura through her office window in *On the Rocks*. The boys in *The Virgin Suicides* spy on the girls through telescopes and binoculars. Surveillance cameras record the Bling Ring burglars. We look – at others and the world – through lenses (individual and cultural) and are looked at – even when, like Charlotte in the opening scene – we are unaware of their gaze.

More fundamentally, to watch *Lost in Translation* and any of Coppola's films is to feel, as Laura Henderson puts it, that we have been cinematic tourists, that we have been transported through space and time to another place.[112] By immersion in an audiovisual experience invoking all our senses (including touch), we feel as though we have actually travelled to Tokyo or Los Angeles, to eighteenth-century Versailles or the Civil War South. On Instagram and Pinterest, social media users post images from *Lost in Translation* as though sharing their own travel snapshots, often with the line, 'I want to go there' – not to Japan, to Coppola's cinematic version. Online sites list the film's locations and travellers post guides to replicating the characters' stay at the Park Hyatt. They drink Suntory or vodka tonics at the New York Bar or order the L.I.T. cocktail, a mix of sake, peach and cherry blossom liqueurs, and cranberry juice, a combination that makes it the colour of Charlotte's panties.

One professional homage recreated the film in miniature, not in Japan but on a soundstage. For the 2018 music video for his song 'Lost in Japan', Canadian singer-songwriter Shawn Mendes cast himself in the role of Bob Harris and Elisha Boe as Charlotte, duplicating the costumes and sets, including the elevator and karaoke booth. Zedd, who produced a remix of the song, has a cameo as Charlie, in their meta staging of the karaoke scene. The video, directed by Jay Martin and shot by Kai Sau, has over one hundred million views on YouTube, augmenting and extending the film's visual legacy. The film's musical legacy equally endures: nearly two decades after its initial release, the original film soundtrack was rereleased on vinyl for a new generation of collectors.

Ironically, a critic in the *Baltimore Sun* had complained, 'The movie registers like a pop song that enters the mind only in fragments because, as a whole, it lacks the style or substance to be memorable.'[113] In fact, *Lost in Translation* is memorable *because* its fragments – its images and music – linger. Travelling across time and around the globe, the film continues to attract new audiences who find style and substance in its music, images and words – even those we cannot hear.

Notes

1 See, for instance, Christopher Shultz, 'What Works & What Doesn't: "Lost in Translation"', LitReactor, 4 September 2015. Available at: <https://litreactor.com/columns/work-non-work-lost-in-translation> (accessed 3 July 2022); Taylor Thomas, 'Screenplay Structure: Lost in Translation', Thomasine Media, 10 June 2019. Available at: <https://www.thomasinemedia.com/post/screenplay-structure-lost-in-translation> (accessed 3 July 2022). For a sustained analysis of how the film resists conventional structuring, as well as art-cinema narration, see Geoff King, *Lost in Translation* (Edinburgh: Edinburgh University Press, 2010), pp. 76–89.

2 It also initiated a pattern that continues in her work, alternating between adapted and original screenplays: her next project, *Marie Antoinette* (2006), an adaptation of a revisionist biography of the queen by Antonia Fraser, was followed by *Somewhere* (2010). *The Bling Ring* (2013), based on a *Vanity Fair* article by Nancy Jo Sales, was followed by an excursus into genre television, *A Very Merry Christmas* (2015). *The Beguiled* (2017) is a doubled adaption: it reworks Thomas Cullinan's 1966 novel, *A Painted Devil*, and responds to Don Siegel's 1971 film adaptation of the same text. It was followed by *On the Rocks* (2020). The director's next project is an adaptation: a limited series for Apple TV+ based on Edith Wharton's *The Custom of the Country*.

3 Quoted in Wendy Mitchell, 'From the iW Vaults | Sofia Coppola Talks "Lost in Translation"', Her Love Story That's Not "Nerdy"', IndieWire, 6 July 2011. Available at: <https://www.indiewire.com/2011/07/from-the-iw-vaults-sofia-coppola-talks-lost-in-translation-her-love-story-thats-not-nerdy-53395/> (accessed 3 July 2022).

4 Joey Nolfi, 'Sofia Coppola: Studio was "Afraid" of Girls Watching *The Virgin Suicides*', *Entertainment Weekly*, 23 April 2018. Available at: <https://ew.com/movies/2018/04/23/sofia-coppola-studio-girls-virgin-suicides/> (accessed 3 July 2022).

5 Quoted in 'Making *Somewhere*', *Somewhere* DVD, dir. Sofia Coppola (Universal City, CA: Focus Features, 2011).

6 Quotations come from the untitled short story.

7 Anne Thompson, 'Tokyo Story: Sofia Coppola's "Lost in Translation"', *Filmmaker: The Magazine of Independent Film* vol. 12 (Autumn 2003). Available at: <https://www.filmmakermagazine.com/archives/issues/fall2003/features/tokyo_story.php> (accessed 3 July 2022).

8 The average length is between 90 and 120 pages, assuming approximately one minute per page.

9 Quoted in Thompson, 'Tokyo Story'.

10 Lynn Hirschberg, 'The Coppola Smart Mob', *New York Times Magazine*, 31 August 2003. Available at: <https://www.nytimes.com/2003/08/31/magazine/the-coppola-smart-mob.html> (accessed 3 July 2022).

11 Thompson, 'Tokyo Story'; Hirschberg, 'Coppola Smart Mob'. Susan Dudley Gold claims Coppola also tried to enlist Al Pacino to act as an intermediary.

See Susan Dudley Gold, *Great Filmmakers: Sofia Coppola* (New York: Cavendish Square, 2015), p. 37.

12 Michael Odmark, 'The Close-Up: Sofia Coppola Talks Filmmaking and *The Beguiled*', FilmLinc Daily, 22 June 2017. Available at: <https://www.filmlinc. org/daily/the-close-up-sofia-coppola-talks-filmmaking-and-the-beguiled/> (accessed 3 July 2022). The director also says that Murray was wearing a seersucker suit, the type he wears in *On the Rocks*.

13 Quoted in Thompson, 'Tokyo Story'.

14 Thompson, 'Tokyo Story'. For a detailed discussion, see Geoff King, *Lost in Translation*, pp. 13–17.

15 Jessica Hundley, 'An Invisible Role', *Los Angeles Times*, 11 September 2003. Available at: <https://www.latimes. com/archives/la-xpm-2003-sep-11-wk-pop11-story.html> (accessed 3 July 2022).

16 Quoted in Meghan Joyce Tozer, 'Interview 3: Mixing Punk Rock, Classical, and New Sounds in Film Music – An Interview with Brian Reitzell', in Liz Greene and Danijela Kulezic-Wilson (eds), *The Palgrave Handbook of Sound Design and Music in Screen Media* (London: Palgrave Macmillan, 2016), pp. 264–5.

17 Sofia Coppola, 'Small Stories #4', in *BEAMS: Beyond Tokyo*, trans. W. David Marx (New York: Rizzoli, 2017), p. 140. Bill Murray wears Fujiwara's Nike Air Woven shoes in 'Dark Mocha' in the hospital scene. See <https:// black-harpoon.medium.com/lost-in-translation-filming-locations-wardrobe-edition-2002-nike-htm-air-woven-rainbow-dark-a61bc6d2e7a2> (accessed 3 July 2022).

18 Quoted in Hirschberg, 'Coppola Smart Mob'.

19 Quoted in Thompson, 'Tokyo Story'.

20 Thompson, 'Tokyo Story'.

21 Geoff King, *Lost in Translation*, p. 12.

22 Polly Vernon, 'Scarlett Fever', *Observer*, 28 December 2003; Joey Nolfi, 'Sofia Coppola Reveals Rashida Jones' Sweet Connection to *Lost in Translation*', *Entertainment Weekly*, 13 August 2020. Available at: <https://ew.com/movies/ sofia-coppola-rashida-jones-lost-in-translation/> (accessed 3 July 2022).

23 Quoted in Thompson, 'Tokyo Story'.

24 Geoff King, *Lost in Translation*, pp. 11–12.

25 Eleanor Coppola, *Notes on a Life* (New York: Applause, 2008), p. 149.

26 Quoted in Hirschberg, 'Coppola Smart Mob'.

27 Tozer, 'Interview with Brian Reitzell', pp. 264–5.

28 Sorina Diaconescu, 'An Upstart, Casual but Confident', *Los Angeles Times*, 7 September 2003. Available at: <https://www.latimes.com/archives/ la-xpm-2003-sep-07-ca-diaconescu7-story.html> (accessed 3 July 2022). For a more detailed analysis of the marketing campaign in relation to indie film practice at the time, see Geoff King, *Lost in Translation*, pp. 16–19.

29 Gold, *Sofia Coppola*, p. 40.

30 Martin A. Grove, 'Focus Heads Focus on "Translation" Success', *Hollywood Reporter*, 10 October 2003.

31 Quoted in Diaconescu, 'Upstart'.

32 According to the Internet Movie Database. Available at: <https://www.

imdb.com/title/tt0335266/business> (accessed 3 July 2022).

33 Geoff King, *Lost in Translation*, p. 23.

34 Ibid., p. 22.

35 Eve Watling, 'The Best Movies of the 2000s, According to Critics', *Newsweek*, 21 August 2018.

36 The title of the article is at odds with the text: Valentina Valentini, '18 of the Best Indie Movies of All Time', *Esquire*, 4 August 2020. Available at: <https://www.esquire.com/uk/culture/film/a32684275/best-indie-movies/> (accessed 3 July 2022).

37 'The 21st Century's 100 Greatest Films', 23 August 2016. Available at: <https://www.bbc.com/culture/story/20160819-the-21st-centurys-100-greatest-films> (accessed 3 July 2022).

38 Some have identified the painting as *Jutta* (1973), which features a female figure in a similar pose but wearing a black negligée and panties. But Coppola pointed to *Maude* (1977) as her reference in an interview with Annette Insdorf for the 92nd Street Y, including an image of Kacere's painting at approximately five minutes in. See 'Sofia Coppola on Filmmaking: A Talk and Q&A with Annette Insdorf', YouTube, 22 April 2020. Available at: <https://www.youtube.com/watch?v=JKj92etN7fw&t=308s> (accessed 3 July 2022).

39 Several film scholars have rejected claims that the image objectifies the female form as Kacere's paintings do, especially given that in Charlotte's later appearances in the same attire, we look with her rather than at her. Lucy Bolton argues, 'her state of undress is not designed to be seen by anyone else, as she is alone in her room. Her solitary, meditative state de-sexualizes her appearance by naturalizing her semi-nudity as the state of dress a woman would be likely to adopt if she was on her own.' See Lucy Bolton, *Film and Female Consciousness: Irigaray, Cinema and Thinking Women* (Basingstoke: Palgrave Macmillan, 2011), pp. 109–10. Fiona Handyside notes that the quasi-still nature of the image disrupts a voyeuristic gaze and that the 'very weight of time pulls [the female figure] from being pure empty iconic spectacle and into the material matter of history itself'. See Fiona Handyside, *Sofia Coppola: A Cinema of Girlhood* (London: I. B. Tauris, 2017), Kindle loc. 375. Also see Todd Kennedy, 'Off with Hollywood's Head: Sofia Coppola as Feminine Auteur', *Film Criticism* vol. 35, no. 1 (Autumn 2010): 45–6; Amy Woodworth, 'A Feminist Theorization of Sofia Coppola's Postfeminist Trilogy', in Marcelline Block (ed.), *Situating the Feminist Gaze and Spectatorship in Postwar Cinema* (Newcastle upon Tyne: Cambridge Scholars Press, 2010), p. 148.

40 The uncredited song contains samples from the following tracks performed by YeLLOW Generation under licence from Defstar Records Inc.: 'LOST Generation', written by Sora Izumikawa; 'Kitakaze To Taiyo', written by Miki Watanabe; and 'CARPE DIEM – Ima Konoshunkanwo Ikiru', written by Akinori Kumata. All lyrics by Masato Ochi.

41 Quoted in Diaconescu, 'Upstart'.

42 Gang of Four, 'Natural's Not in It', written by Dave Allen, Hugo Burnham,

Andrew Gill and Jon King, released 1979 by Warner Bros. Records/EMI.

43 Quoted in Alexander Ballinger, *New Cinematographers* (New York: Collins Design, 2004), p. 31.

44 Quoted in Diaconescu, 'Upstart'.

45 In the short story, Bob stays on the 54th floor and Charlotte on the 56th, but in reality the bar occupies the top floor – the 52nd.

46 Lucy Bolton offers a compelling reading of the scene, noting that it emphasises Charlotte's 'quieter, subdued, and rather serious world of observation', adding that it frames her as an explorer. See Bolton, *Film and Female Consciousness*, pp. 106–10.

47 Such details, combined with the fact that Johansson resembles Coppola and adopted her personal style for Charlotte, prompted speculation at the time that the film was a *roman à clef* about the director's marriage to Spike Jonze, whom she divorced two months after the film's release. See, for instance, Hirschberg, 'Coppola Smart Mob'.

48 In the shooting script, the scene appears far earlier, again revealing how editing contributed to the film's emotional power. Placed earlier, it would have appeared as merely expository rather than as cementing the intimate connection already forged cinematically via image.

49 Coppola had seen Catherine Lambert perform at the hotel in Tokyo in 2001. A year later, her producer Ross Katz tracked Lambert down in South Australia and invited her to play the part of the singer.

50 The film, centred on Marcello Mastroianni's peregrinations through Rome, offers a cinematic parallel to the couple's night-time adventures in Tokyo, which are discussed in the next chapter.

51 Anna Backman Rogers cleverly makes the association: Bob is in a 'relationship of prostitution with Suntory'. See Anna Backman Rogers, *Sofia Coppola: The Politics of Visual Pleasure* (New York and Oxford: Berghahn, 2019), p. 79.

52 For a translation of the scene, see Motoko Rich, 'What Else Was Lost in Translation', *New York Times*, 21 September 2003. Available at: <https://www.nytimes.com/2003/09/21/style/what-else-was-lost-in-translation.html> (accessed 3 July 2022).

53 The 'broadcast' version of the fictional show is included on the DVD.

54 A contributor to the 'Trivia' section on IMDb identifies it as 'Ghost in the Shell'. Scarlett Johansson starred in a film adaptation of the comic in 2017.

55 Coppola, quoted in Gold, *Sofia Coppola*, p. 24.

56 Roxy Music, 'More Than This', written by Bryan Ferry, released 1982, published by BMG Rights Management Limited. While the actors were allowed to choose their own songs, Coppola picked this for Bill Murray, knowing he would struggle to hit the high notes. See Tozer, 'Interview with Brian Reitzell', p. 265.

57 Charlotte's amateur version of 'Brass in Pocket' also contrasts with the strippers at Orange who perform to a Peaches song that includes the line, 'Check out my Chrissie be-Hynde'.

58 The opening drum riff is taken from The Ronettes' 'Be My Baby'. When working from the script, Reitzell originally wanted to use the song earlier, in place of 'Sometime', for the cab ride back to the hotel, before Bob carries Charlotte down the hallway, but changed his mind once he tried it with the ending. 'I remember trying it at the end with Sofia at my house,' he recalls. 'I only had it as a record, so I'm just dropping the needle while we're watching a little VHS tape. But when that thing hit, it was just perfect.' See Tozer, 'Interview with Brian Reitzell', p. 267.

59 The Jesus and Mary Chain, 'Just Like Honey', written by James McLeish Reid and William Reid, released September 1985, published by Chrysalis Music and WB Music Corp.

60 The film's music supervisor Brian Reitzell performed on the drums and Coppola later directed the music video for the song, which includes footage from *Lost in Translation* that does not appear in the final cut.

61 Kevin Shields, 'City Girl', written by Kevin Shields, recorded summer 2002, released 2003 by Inertia (Australia)/ Emperor Norton Records.

62 One translation can be found online at: <https://japanoscope.com/kaze-wo-atsumete-lyrics/> (accessed 3 July 2022). The accompanying interpretation notes that the Tokyo of the song 'is an imaginary city existing in dream and memory'.

63 Anna Backman Rogers offers a compelling Sartrean reading, noting, 'the film's action hinges on what *does not happen* between them, what remains unarticulated and impossible'. See Backman Rogers, *Sofia Coppola*, p. 85.

64 Coppola, *Notes on a Life*, p. 187.

65 Peter Bradshaw, '*Lost in Translation* Review', *Guardian*, 8 January 2004. Available at: <https://www.theguardian.com/film/2004/jan/09/lost-in-translation-review> (accessed 3 July 2022).

66 Lisa Schwarzbaum, 'Lost in Translation', *Entertainment Weekly*, 11 September 2003. Available at: <https://ew.com/article/2003/09/11/lost-translation-2/> (accessed 3 July 2022).

67 Mark Caro, '"Lost" and Found', *Chicago Tribune*, 12 September 2003.

68 Scott Foundas, 'More Than This', *Los Angeles Weekly*, 11 September 2003. Available at: <https://www.laweekly.com/more-than-this/> (accessed 3 July 2022).

69 Kenneth Turan, 'Bill at His Best', *Los Angeles Times*, 12 September 2003. Available at: <https://www.latimes.com/archives/la-xpm-2003-sep-12-et-turan12-story.html> (accessed 3 July 2022).

70 David Edelstein, 'Movie Review: "Lost in Translation"', Fresh Air, 12 September 2003. Available at: <https://freshairarchive.org/segments/movie-review-lost-translation> (accessed 3 July 2022).

71 David Ansen, 'Scarlett Fever', *Newsweek*, 14 September 2003. Available at: <https://www.newsweek.com/scarlett-fever-136731> (accessed 3 July 2022); Desson Howe, '"Lost in Translation" Finds the Right Words',

Washington Post, 12 September 2003. Available at: <https://www.washingtonpost.com/archive/lifestyle/2003/09/12/lost-in-translation-finds-the-right-words/de74cb29-2cf7-4d87-b313-0f6d2b4768b8/> (accessed 3 July 2022).

72 David Rooney, 'Lost in Translation', *Variety*, 31 August 2003. Available at: <https://variety.com/2003/film/awards/lost-in-translation-6-1200539681/> (accessed 3 July 2022); Joe Morgenstern, 'Nothing Lost in "Translation": Tale of Unlikely Pair in Tokyo Is Giddy, Witty and Wise', *Wall Street Journal*, 12 September 2003. Available at: <https://www.wsj.com/articles/SB106333243195535800> (accessed 3 July 2022).

73 Nathan Rabin, 'Lost in Translation', AV Club, 9 September 2003. Available at: <https://www.avclub.com/lost-in-translation-1798198878> (accessed 3 July 2022); Peter Rainer, 'Sleepless in Tokyo', *New York*, 4 September 2003. Available at: <https://nymag.com/nymetro/movies/reviews/n_9178/> (accessed 3 July 2022).

74 Elvis Mitchell, 'An American in Japan Making a Connection', *New York Times*, 12 September 2003. Available at: <https://www.nytimes.com/2003/09/12/movies/film-review-an-american-in-japan-making-a-connection.html> (accessed 3 July 2022).

75 'A Conversation with Bill Murray and Sofia Coppola', Rome, 19 October 2003, *Lost in Translation*, DVD Extra.

76 Stephanie Zacharek, '"Lost in Translation"', *Salon*, 12 September 2003. Available at: <https://www.salon.com/2003/09/12/translation/> (accessed 3 July 2022).

77 Richard Corliss, 'A Victory for Lonely Hearts', *Time*, 8 September 2003. Available at: <https://content.time.com/time/magazine/article/0,9171,483290,00.html> (accessed 3 July 2022).

78 Roger Ebert, '*Lost in Translation*', RogerEbert.com, 12 September 2003. Available at: <https://www.rogerebert.com/reviews/lost-in-translation-2003> (accessed 3 July 2022).

79 Stephen Hunter, '"Lost in Translation": Bonds Without Borders', *Washington Post*, 12 September 2003. Available at: <https://www.washingtonpost.com/archive/lifestyle/2003/09/12/lost-in-translation-bonds-without-borders/1f4bf5c4-e3fb-4d46-91f4-fbb8951a86ec/> (accessed 3 July 2022).

80 David Denby, 'Heartbreak Hotels', *New Yorker*, 7 September 2003. Available at: <https://www.newyorker.com/magazine/2003/09/15/heartbreak-hotels> (accessed 3 July 2022).

81 Edelstein, 'Review'.

82 Ken Fox, 'Lost in Translation Reviews', *TV Guide*. Available at: <https://www.tvguide.com/movies/lost-in-translation/review/2030098585/> (accessed 3 July 2022).

83 Corliss, 'Victory'.

84 Mairead Small Staid, 'Fifteen Years Later, Still *Lost in Translation*', Jezebel, 12 November 2018. Available at: <https://jezebel.com/fifteen-years-later-still-lost-in-translation-1830308411> (accessed 3 July 2022).

85 Carrie Rickey, 'A Tender, Sincere Bill Murray: In Sofia Coppola's "Lost in Translation", He Finds His Role of a Lifetime', *Philadelphia Inquirer*, 19 September 2003. Available at: <https://www.inquirer.com/philly/entertainment/movies/MovieReviewID_20030919_inq_weekend_CRKLOST.html> (accessed 3 July 2022).

86 Paul Julian Smith, 'Tokyo Drifters', *Sight and Sound* vol. 14, no. 1 (January 2004): 13–16, 15.

87 Maria San Filippo, *Cineaste* vol. 29, no. 1 (Winter 2003): 26–8, 28.

88 Frank P. Tomasulo, 'Japan Through Others' Lenses: *Hiroshima Mon Amour* (1959) and *Lost in Translation* (2003)', *Japan Studies Review* vol. 11 (2007): 143–56, 151.

89 Homay King, 'Lost in Translation', *Film Quarterly* vol. 59, no. 1 (Autumn 2005): 45–8, 45, 48.

90 Alice Lovejoy, 'Two Lost Souls Adrift in Tokyo Forge an Unlikely Bond in Sofia Coppola's 21st-Century Brief Encounter', *Film Comment* vol. 39, no. 4 (July/August 2003): 11.

91 Inkoo Kang, '*Lost in Translation* Is an Insufferable, Racist Mess – Why Would We Expect *The Beguiled* to Be Any Different?', *MTV News*, 20 June 2017. Available at: <https://www.mtv.com/news/3021638/lost-in-translation-is-an-insufferable-racist-mess-why-would-we-expect-the-beguiled-to-be-any-different/> (accessed 3 July 2022); Georgie Carr, 'An Unwavering Self-Regard: Sofia Coppola's "On The Rocks" (2020)', *Another Gaze*, 16 November 2020. Available at: <https://www.anothergaze.com/unwavering-self-regard-sofia-coppolas-rocks-2020/> (accessed 3 July 2022).

92 Lucy Bolton, 'Sofia Coppola's *Lost in Translation*: Liminality, Loneliness, and Learning from an-Other', in Suzanne Ferriss (ed.), *The Bloomsbury Handbook to Sofia Coppola* (London and New York: Bloomsbury, 2023), p. 41.

93 Todd McGowan, 'There Is Nothing *Lost in Translation*', *Quarterly Review of Film and Video* vol. 24 (2007): 59; Sharon Lin Tay, *Women on the Edge: Twelve Political Film Practices* (New York: Palgrave Macmillan, 2009), p. 139. Also see Geoff King, *Lost in Translation*, pp. 131–5.

94 Quoted in Homay King, 'Lost in Translation', p. 45.

95 Fumie Nakamura, 'A Sampling of Japanese Comment on "Lost in Translation"', UCLA Center for Chinese Studies, 11 June 2004. Available at: <https://www.international.ucla.edu/ccs/article/11981> (accessed 3 July 2022).

96 The organisation is now defunct and the original text is no longer accessible.

97 Michael Richardson, *Otherness in Hollywood Cinema* (New York and London: Continuum, 2010), pp. 170–1.

98 Coppola, *Notes on a Life*, p. 193.

99 Peter Travers, 'Lost in Translation', *Rolling Stone*, 8 September 2003, p. 4. Available at: <https://www.rollingstone.com/tv-movies/tv-movie-reviews/lost-in-translation-127187/> (accessed 3 July 2022).

100 Zack Sharf, '"Lost In Translation", 15 Years Later: Sofia Coppola on Ending the Film on Her Terms and the Year It Took to Cast Bill Murray', *IndieWire*, 27 August 2018. Available at: <https://www.indiewire.com/2018/08/lost-in-translation-15th-anniversary-sofia-coppola-interview-ending-

whisper-meaning-1201998010/>
(accessed 3 July 2022).

101 Sangeeta Singh-Kurtz, 'Why Is
Scarlett Johansson Always in Sad
Divorce Movies?', *The Cut*, 4 January
2020. Available at: <https://www.thecut.
com/2020/01/marriage-story-scarlett-
johanssons-divorce-movies.html>
(accessed 3 July 2022).

102 Steven Kurutz, 'The Peculiar Ascent
of Bill Murray to Secular Saint', *New York
Times*, 30 November 2015. Available at:
<https://www.nytimes.com/2015/12/04/
fashion/mens-style/the-peculiar-
ascent-of-bill-murray-to-secular-saint.
html> (accessed 3 July 2022).

103 Mitchell, 'An American in Japan'.

104 'A Conversation with Bill Murray
and Sofia Coppola'.

105 'Roddy Doyle Scored 8 Out of 10
on a Quiz about Roddy Doyle', *New
York Times*, 25 June 2020. Available at:
<https://www.nytimes.com/2020/06/25/
books/review/roddy-doyle-by-the-book-
interview.html> (accessed 3 July 2022).

106 Manohla Dargis, '"On the Rocks"
Review: Daddy Dearest and His Late
Bloomer', *New York Times*, 1 October
2020. Available at: <https://www.
nytimes.com/2020/10/01/movies/
on-the-rocks-review.html> (accessed
3 July 2022).

107 Frank Mojica, 'Cinema Sounds:
Lost in Translation', Consequence,
26 May 2010. Available at: <https://
consequence.net/2010/05/cinema-
sounds-lost-in-translation/> (accessed
3 July 2022).

108 Jon Dolan, Will Hermes, Christian
Hoard and Rob Sheffield, 'The 25
Greatest Soundtracks of All Time:
From "Easy Rider" to "A Hard Day's
Night"', *Rolling Stone*, 29 August 2013.
Available at: <https://www.rollingstone.
com/movies/movie-lists/the-25-
greatest-soundtracks-of-all-time-41108/
head-1968-220556/> (accessed 3 July
2022); 'The 50 Best Movie Soundtracks
of All Time', *Pitchfork*, 19 February
2019. Available at: <https://pitchfork.
com/features/lists-and-guides/the-50-
best-movie-soundtracks-of-all-time/>
(accessed 3 July 2022). *Lost in Translation*
comes in at #7, besting *Marie Antoinette*
(#36).

109 See Coppola, *Notes on a Life*, p. 276.

110 'Japandering' is shorthand for
Western stars who cash in on their
stardom by advertising products in
Japan.

111 The line appears in 'Little Gidding',
the final poem of Eliot's *Four Quartets*
(London: Faber and Faber, 1942).

112 She does so with far greater
sophistication and complexity than
I can represent here: see Laura
Henderson, 'Psychogeography and
Cinema(car)tography: Cinematic
Tourism and Sofia Coppola's Films',
in Ferriss (ed.), *Bloomsbury Handbook to
Sofia Coppola*, pp. 355–70.

113 Michael Sragow, 'Spirituality Gets
Lost in "Translation": Character Duet
Fails to Connect', *Baltimore Sun*,
19 September 2003, p. 1E.

Credits

Lost in Translation
USA/Japan
2003

Written and Directed by
Sofia Coppola
Produced by
Ross Katz
Sofia Coppola
Director of Photography
Lance Acord
Editor
Sarah Flack
Costume Designer
Nancy Steiner
Production Designers
Anne Ross
K. K. Barrett
Line Producer
Callum Greene
Music Producer
Brian Reitzell
Sound Designer
Richard Beggs

© 2003 Lost in
Translation Inc.

Production Companies
Focus Features
Tohokushinsha
American Zoetrope
Elemental Films

Executive Producers
Francis Ford Coppola
Fred Roos
Associate Producer
Mitch Glazer
First Assistant Director
Takahide Kawakami

Co-producer
Stephen Schible
Additional Japanese Unit
Roman Coppola
Line Producer (Japan)
Kiyoshi Inoue
Chief Assistant Director
Hiroya Igawa
Second Assistant Director
Taiichi Sugiyama
Second Second Assistant Directors
Motonobu Kato
Shu Fujimoto
Production Supervisor
Anthony G. Katagas
Production Office Coordinator
Kazuko Shingyoku
Production Coordinator
Masahiro Yoshikawa
Assistant Production Office Coordinators
Masako Matsumura
Ai Ichiki
Office Production Assistants
Hitoshi Abe
Maremi Watanabe
Taro Miyake
Production Consultant
Hiroko Kawasaki
Product Placement Coordinator
Ashley Bearden
Japanese Casting
Ryoichi Kondo

Additional Japanese Casting
Stephanie Hayman
Casting Assistants
Hauko Sone
Daiki Chiba
Akira Yamaguchi
Hiroto Nakagaki
Casting PA
Miwa Sakaguchi
Production Accountant (Japan)
Natsuko Nezu
Assistant to Natsuko Nezu
Tomoko Kojima
Production Accountant (US)
John Finn
Script Supervisor
Eva Z. Cabrera
Script Translation
Kimiko Onishi
Assistant Editor
Jamie Kirkpatrick
Additional Assistant Editor
Susan Finch
Editing Facilities
Red Car Post:
Jennifer Letterman
First Assistant Camera
Mark Williams
Second Assistant Camera
Takuro Ishizaka
Loader
Takuji Murata
Camera Operator
Lance Acord

Additional First Assistant
Nobuko Uranishi

Additional Second Assistant
Yasushi Miyata

Still Photography
Yoshio Sato

Camera Equipment
Clairmont Camera (LA)

Production Sound Mixer
Drew Kunin

Boom Operator
Kira Smith

Dailies Synching
Sound Design Yurta Inc.

Gaffer
Yuji Wada

Best Boy Electrician #1
Yoshio Ishikawa

Best Boy Electrician #2
Michiaki Kamochi

Electricians
Masayuki Nishimura
Takeshi Kagami

Key Grip
Satoshi Tsuyuki

Best Boy Grip
Akira Kanno

Art Director
Mayumi Tomita

Assistant Art Directors
Ryo Sugimoto
Momoko Nakamura

Art Department Coordinator
Rika Nakanishi

Leadman
Toru Takahashi

Set Decorators
Towako Kuwajima
Tomomi Nishio

Assistant Set Decorators
Tomiko Ishiyama
Hitomi Nimura

Additional Assistant Set Decorators
Ryo Nobuka
Takahiro Kikuchi

Property Master
Keisuke Sakurai

Assistant Property Master
Chie Che

Assistant Designer
Michelle Tomaszewski

Wardrobe Supervisors
Anita Brown
Haruka Takahashi

Set Costumer
Masae Sakurai

Bilingual Assistant
Yoko Takeuchi

Wardrobe Supervisor (Kyoto)
Noriko Hattori

Key Hair and Make-up Artist
Morag Ross

Hair/Make-up
Akemi

Assistant Hair/Make-up
Yoko Sato
Fukushi Kawata

Unit/Key Location Manager
Keizo Shukuzaki

Location Coordinator
Mikiko Anzai

Assistant Location Manager
Takuya Kaneko

Key Set PA
Hiroshi Harada

Set PAs
Tomohiko Seki
Toji Hirano

Location Manager (Kyoto)
Kiyoshi Kurokawa

Bilingual Coordinator
Brian Kobo

Bilingual Assistants
Yumiko Sekiguchi
Katumi Nakane
Eriko Miyagawa
Hirohito Gotou

Stunt Coordination
Hirofumi Nakase

Drivers
Eiji Fujii
Akira Ebata
Sakae Kaminaka
Minoru Tsuruno
Tomoo Senuma
Kiyotaka Inagaki

Additional Drivers
Yuki Shimizu
Osamu Sasaki

Assistant to Ross Katz
Jonathan Ferrantelli

Assistant to Sofia Coppola
Susan Herbert

Assistants to Bill Murray
Kumi Tanaka
Koichi Tanaka

**Assistant to
Scarlett Johansson**
Naoki Takagi
**Assistant to
Giovanni Ribisi
and Anna Faris**
Sayuri Kanamori
**Legal Services
Provided by**
Epstein, Levinsohn,
Bodine, Hurwitz and
Weinstein LLP:
Susan H. Bodine
Andrea Cannistraci
Alison Cohen
Armstrong Hirsch
Jackoway Tyerman &
Wertheimer:
George T. Hayum
Barry W. Tyerman
**Production Attorney
(Japan)**
Atsushi Naito Esq.
**Insurance by Dennis
Reiff & Associates**
Dennis Reiff
Ross Miller
**Additional Insurance
(Japan)**
Ryu Insurance Agency
Co., Ltd.
Researcher
Shari Chertok
TV Clip Editor
Howard Shur
Karaoke Video Editor
Yuji Oshige
**Karaoke Camera
Operator**
Anne Rice

**Supervising Sound
Editor**
Michael Kirchberger
ADR/Dialogue Editor
David Cohen
FX Editor
Julia Shirar
Additional ADR Editors
Deborah Wallach
George Berndt
Assistant Sound Editor
Everett Moore
Sound Intern
Matthew Hartman
Music Editor
Richard Beggs
Foley Supervisor
William Storkson
Foley Recordist
Jory K. Prum
Foley Artist
Marnie Moore
Re-recording Mixers
Richard Beggs
Kent Sparling
Re-recording Supervisor
Robert Knox
Recordist
Glenn Kasprzycki
**Re-recording
Engineering**
Brian Sarvis
**American Zoetrope
Mix Facility Manager**
Howard Stein
**American Zoetrope
Post-production**
Kim Aubry
**Mix Facility
Coordination**
James Levine

Mix Facility Support
Dawn Angel
Ethan Derner
Dolby Engineer
Dan Sperry
Payroll Services
Entertainment Partners
**Post-production
Accounting**
JFA Inc.
Title Design
Miles Murray Sorrell
FUEL
Opticals
Title House Digital
Gray Matter
Negative Matched by
West Coast Editorial:
Heidi Zellner
**Film Developing and
Dailies**
Imagica, Tokyo
Post-Lab
FotoKem Laboratory
Timer
Bob Fredrickson
Production Financing
Natexis Banques
Populaires:
Bennett Pozil
Bond Company
Film Finances Inc.:
Kurt Woolner
Greg Trattner
Maureen Duffy
Original Music by
Kevin Shields
'Alone in Kyoto' by
Air

Additional Music by
Brian Reitzell
Roger Joseph Manning Jr
William Storkson
Music Clearances
Jill Meyers
Soundtrack
'Girls', written by Tim
Holmes and Richard
McGuire, performed
by Death In Vegas;
'Minuetto', written by
Dominic Sands; 'The
Thrill Is Gone', written
by Roy Hawkins and
Rick Darnell, performed
by Catherine Lambert;
'Fantino', written and
performed by Sébastian
Tellier; 'Torn Into',
written by Matt Sims,
performed by Mount
Sims; 'Scarborough Fair/
Canticle', written by
Paul Simon and Arthur
Garfunkel, performed
by Catherine Lambert;
'Blue Atmosphere',
written by Francesco
Santucci, Antonello
Vannucchi, Giorgio
Rosciglione; 'Love Gun',
written and performed
by Rick James; 'Muyu',
written and performed
by Des-Row Union; 'You
Stepped Out of a Dream',
written by Gus Kahn
and Nacio Herb Brown,
performed by Catherine

Lambert; 'Tommib',
written by Tom
Jenkinson, performed
by Squarepusher; 'The
State We're In', written
by Tom Rowlands and Ed
Simons, performed by
The Chemical Brothers;
'She Gets Around',
written by Jason Falkner,
Roger Joseph Manning
Jr and Brian Reitzell,
performed by TV Eyes;
'Feeling I Get', written by
Mike Brewer, performed
by Mary Butterworth
Group; 'Tomei Tengu
BGM', written and
performed by Takeo
Watanabe; 'Too Young',
written and performed
by Phoenix; 'God Save
the Queen', written by
Paul Cook, Steve Jones,
John Lydon and Glen
Matlock, performed
by Fumihiro Hayashi;
'(What's So Funny
'Bout) Peace, Love and
Understanding', written
by Nick Lowe, performed
by Bill Murray; 'Brass
in Pocket', written by
Chrissie Hynde and
James Honeyman-Scott,
performed by Scarlett
T. Johansson; 'More
Than This', written by
Bryan Ferry, performed
by Bill Murray; 'Kaze

Wo Atsumete', written
by Takashi Matsumoto
and Haruomi Hosono,
performed by Shigekazu
Aida, performed by
Happy End; 'Sometimes',
written by Kevin Shields,
performed by My Bloody
Valentine; 'Fuck the
Pain Away', written and
performed by Peaches;
'Nobody Does It Better',
written by Marvin
Hamlisch and Carole
Bayer Sager, performed
by Anna Faris; 'Alone in
Kyoto', written by Nicolas
Godin and Jean-Benoît
Dunckle, performed
by Air; 'Midnight at
the Oasis', written
by David Nichtern,
performed by Catherine
Lambert; 'So into You',
written by Buddy Buie,
Robert Nix and Dean
Daughtry, performed
by Mark Willms; 'Just
Like Honey', written by
James McLeish Reid and
William Reid, performed
by The Jesus and Mary
Chain; 'La Dolce Vita',
written and performed
by Nino Rota
**Soundtrack Available
on**
Emperor Norton Records

Thank You
Bart Walker, Roman, Steph, Kun, Zoe and Xan, Gretta Seacat, Susan Herbert, Chris Neil, Josh Hartnett, John Lydon, Hiroko, Marc Jacobs International, Kate Waters, Robert and Stacey, Keanu Reeves, Erwin Stoff, Anna Sui, The Directors Bureau, Mom and Dad, Spike, Rima Acord, Wes Anderson, Kelly Lynch, Jean Touitou, A.P.C., Anton Kawasaki, Paul Simon and Eddie Simon, Joe Dapello, Jessica Tuchinsky, David Russell and Janet Grillo, Lorne Michaels, Jack Sullivan, Peter Miles, Mathew Minami, Helmut Lang, Staff of Park Hyatt Tokyo, Nobuhiko Kitamura, Hysteric Glamour, Toshinari Takahashi, C.I.A. Co., Ltd., Suntory Limited, Tatsuya Matsui, Yomiuru Telecasting Corp., Masatoshi Nagase, Akira Okano, Hiroshi Kunimasa, Forest Corporation, Inc., Takuo Yasuda, Yuji Sadai, Tetsurou Yoshida, Pat Lucas, Brad Rosenberger, Damon Murray, Stephen Sorrell

Mr Murray's Wardrobe Provided by
Helmut Lang
Park Hyatt Tokyo
Hiroshi Fujiwara, Nobuaki Okaji, Head Porter, Head Porter Plus, Goodenough
Mathew's Best Hit TV
Hiroaki Nishimura, Masaki Takahashi, Hidesuke Kataoka, Aya Furuse, Sinji Nishigaki, Minako Yoshii, Shinichi Matsumoto, Tomoaki Shiono, Yukio Tsutsumimoto, Kozo Komurasaki, Tsukasa Yosuke Imataki, Tadahito Kawada, Toshihide Saito, Akihiko Okamoto, Takao Yamamoto
TV Asahi
Yoshimoto Kogyo Co., Ltd.
Location Support
Tokyo Medical University Hospital, Sputnik Pad/ Idee, Tabloid News Clothe to You, Jogan-ji Temple, Kawaguchiko Country Club, Ichikan Sushi, Parlor Botan, Air/Daikinyama, Hysteric Glamour, Heian-jingu Shrine, Nanzen-ji Temple, Tokyu Corporation, Central Japan Railway Company
Product Support
JAL, Namco Limited, Konami, SEGA

Corporation, Hello Kitty, Sanrio Co., Ltd., Artist International Ingram Co., Ltd., Mon Seuil Co., Ltd., San-X Co., Ltd., Switch Publishing, Studio Voice, Little More, Rockin' on Japan, Cut, Monthly Magazine Inu No Kimochi (Benesse), Neko Publishing Co., Ltd., Shogakukan Big Comic Superior, Plus Eighty One/D.D. Wave Co., Ltd., Magazine House, Daiichikosho Co., Ltd., Ozeki Corporation, Pizza of Death Records, Inou ID by Shiseido, Pentax Corporation, Ikegami Tsushinki Co., Ltd., Toraya Confectionery Co., Ltd., Audio-Technica, Kyocera Corporation, Actus, Minato Shokai Co., Ltd., Daiko, House Styling (Dinos), Apple Macintosh
Wardrobe Support
A Bathing Ape, Head Porter, MilkFed, XLARGE®, Cord Three Co., Ltd., Cos-Mo-Ra-Ma, Sage de Cret, Pas de Alais, So, Daniel Cremieux, Kimono Rakya, Remake©T-K, Georg Jensen Japan Ltd., Abiste, Chrome Hearts, Boutique Osaki, Nîme de Blue, Ap-ron, Mimore, Muji, Agnes B.,

Nice Collective, Puma, Lacoste, Propaganda, Mia & Lizzy, Plein Sud, Vans, Juicy, Clarks, TSE, Bobby Jones, Mahna Mahna, Levi's, Cosabella, Passionbait, Arak's Modern Amusement, Saffilo, Eres, Cutler & Gross, Persol, M.R.S.

Additional Support
Shipping Provided by
JMSA Logistics:
Tony Adrid

Shibuya Jumbo Monitor
Leased by
QFRONT

Billboard and Ad Truck
Provided by
ADMAX Co., Ltd.

Crew Accommodations
Oakwood Residence Aoyama

Air Transportation
Japan Airlines

Camera Accessories
Rentals
Eizo Service Co., Ltd.
Shineo Camera
Grip Equipment
Tokky's Union Paradise
Electric Equipment
Kurosawa Film Studios Inc.

Kyoto Production
Eizo Kyoto Co.
Kansai Location Service Co.

Production Office
Cleaning
Yamatsu Services

Production Office
Security
SECOM, Inc.

Film Stock
Kodak Japan Ltd.

Walkies Rental
On the Way, Inc.

Production Vehicles
Fuji Movie, Inc.
Air Support
Concord Inc.
Nouvelle Vague Co., Ltd.

Strobe Lights
Provided by
Broncolor Agai Trading Corporation

Posy Robot
SGI Japan Ltd.
Flower Robotics, Inc.

TV CLIPS
MTV Station Promo
with VJ Grover
Courtesy of MTV Japan, Kabushiki Kaisya

Shinshutsudoi Miniska
Police: Episodes 294
and 303
Courtesy of C.I.A., Co., Ltd

Shiritsutantei Hama
Mike: Episode 11
Courtesy of Yomiuri Telecasting Corporation

Hanagoyomi
Courtesy of Forest Corporation, Inc.

Chillsphere 001 Flow
Courtesy of Masashi Kitazato, Tsutomu Shimada, Buddhastick Transparent

Tomei Tengu
Courtesy © of Kadokawa-Daiei Pictures, Inc.

Saturday Night Live
Courtesy of Broadway Video Enterprises and NBC Studios

La Dolce Vita
Courtesy of International Media Films, Inc./Third Millennium Films, Inc.
Courtesy of Ms Anita Ekberg and the estate of Marcello Mastroianni
Courtesy of Pathé Films

CAST
Scarlett Johansson
Charlotte

Bill Murray
Bob Harris

Akiko Takeshita
Ms Kawasaki

Kazuyoshi
Minamimagoe
press agent

Kazuko Shibata
press agent

Take
press agent

Ryuichiro Baba
concierge

Akira Yamaguchi
bellboy

Catherine Lambert
jazz singer

François du Bois
Sausalito piano

Tim Leffman
Sausalito guitar

Gregory Pekar
American businessman #1
Richard Allen
American businessman #2
Giovanni Ribisi
John
Yutaka Tadokoro
commercial director
Jun Maki
Suntory client
Nao Asuka
Premium Fantasy woman
Tetsuro Naka
stills photographer
Kanako Nakazato
make-up person
Fumihiro Hayashi
Charlie
Hiroko Kawasaki
Hiroko
Daikon
Bambie
Anna Faris
Kelly
Asuka Shimuzu
Kelly's translator
Ikuko Takahashi
ikebana instructor
Koichi Tanaka
bartender, NY Bar
Hugo Codaro
aerobics instructor
Akiko Monou
P Chan
Akimitsu Naruyama
French Japanese nightclub patron

Hiroshi Kawashima
bartender, nightclub
Hiromix
Hiromix
Nobuhiko Kitamura
Nobu
Nao Kitman
Nao
Akira
Hans
Kunichi Nomura
Kun
Yasuhiko Hattori
Charlie's friend
Shigekazu Aida
Mr Valentine
Kazuo Yamada
hospital receptionist
Akira Motomura
old man
Osamu Shigematu
doctor
Mathew Minami
TV host
Kei Takyo
TV translator
Ryo Kondo
politician
Yumi Ikeda
politician's aide
Yumika Saki
politician's aide
Yuji Okabe
politician's aide
Dietrich Bollmann
German hotel guest
Georg O. P. Eschert
German hotel guest
Mark Willms
Carl West

Lisle Wilkerson
sexy businesswoman
Blake Crawford
stand-in for Mr Murray
Angela Panetta
stand-in for Ms Johansson

Production Details
Production began
29 September 2002.
Shot on location in
Tokyo and Kyoto, Japan.
Colour
35mm
1.85:1
Running time:
102 minutes

Release Details
US theatrical release
on 3 October 2003
Premieres: Telluride
Film Festival (29 August
2003), Venice Film
Festival (31 August 2003),
Toronto Film Festival
(5 September 2003);
LA and NY openings
(12 September 2003)

Bibliography

Backman Rogers, Anna, 'Lost in Translation (2003)', in *Sofia Coppola: The Politics of Visual Pleasure* (New York and Oxford: Berghahn, 2019), pp. 69–89.

Bolton, Lucy, 'Lost in Translation: The Potential of Becoming', *Film and Female Consciousness: Irigaray, Cinema and Thinking Women* (Basingstoke: Palgrave Macmillan, 2011), pp. 95–127.

Bolton, Lucy, 'Sofia Coppola's *Lost in Translation*: Liminality, Loneliness, and Learning from an-Other', in Suzanne Ferriss (ed.), *The Bloomsbury Handbook to Sofia Coppola* (London and New York: Bloomsbury, 2023), pp. 35–49.

Cook, Pam, 'Sofia Coppola', in Yvonne Tasker (ed.), *Fifty Contemporary Film Directors*, 2nd edn (Oxford and London: Routledge, 2011), pp. 126–34.

Ferriss, Suzanne, *The Cinema of Sofia Coppola: Fashion, Culture and Celebrity* (London and New York: Bloomsbury, 2021).

Handyside, Fiona, *Sofia Coppola: A Cinema of Girlhood* (London: I. B. Tauris, 2017).

Kennedy, Todd, 'Off with Hollywood's Head: Sofia Coppola as Feminine Auteur', *Film Criticism* vol. 35, no. 1 (Autumn 2010): 37–59.

King, Geoff, *Lost in Translation* (Edinburgh: Edinburgh University Press, 2010).

King, Homay, *Lost in Translation: Orientalism, Cinema, and the Enigmatic Signifier* (Durham, NC, and London: Duke University Press, 2010).

McGowan, Todd, 'There Is Nothing Lost in Translation', *Quarterly Review of Film and Video* vol. 24 (2007): 53–63.

Smaill, Belinda, 'Sofia Coppola: Reading the Director', *Feminist Media Studies* vol. 13, no. 1 (2013): 148–62.

Smith, Jeff, 'Our Lives in Pink: Sofia Coppola as Transmedia Audiovisual Stylist', in Carol Vernallis, Holly Rogers and Lisa Perrott (eds), *Transmedia Directors: Artistry, Industry and New Audiovisual Aesthetics* (London: Bloomsbury, 2019), pp. 75–91.

Tay, Sharon Lin, *Women on the Edge: Twelve Political Film Practices* (New York: Palgrave Macmillan, 2009), pp. 126–47.

Woodworth, Amy, 'A Feminist Theorization of Sofia Coppola's Postfeminist Trilogy', in Marcelline Block (ed.), *Situating the Feminist Gaze and Spectatorship in Postwar Cinema* (Newcastle upon Tyne: Cambridge Scholars Press, 2010), pp. 138–67.

Wyatt, Justin, *The Virgin Suicides: Reverie, Sorrow and Young Love* (New York and London: Routledge, 2019).